The

in Ireland

In memory of
George O'Malley
who taught us all so much

The Best of
Wine
in Ireland

Jacinta Delahaye

With a foreword
by
T. P. Whelehan

A. & A. Farmar

British Library Cataloguing in Publication data
A CIP catalogue record for this book is available from
the British Library.

Cover design by Bluett
Cover photograph Ronan O'Raw
Proof-reading Pat Carroll
Design and typesetting A. & A. Farmar
Printed and bound by Betaprint

ISBN 1 899047 08 5

Published by
A. & A. Farmar
Beech House
78 Ranelagh Village
Dublin 6

Contents

The Wines

Acknowledgements

The author and publishers would like to thank the many people whose generosity and enthusiastic commitment made the guide possible.

• Our tasting panel, who gave generously and voluntarily of their expertise and time, though we hope they had fun too: the glorious summer of 1995 witnessed some hugely enjoyable *al fresco* lunches where the highlights of the morning's tasting were lingered over and savoured in the best possible circumstances—with good company and good food.

• The wine importers, who supplied samples for tasting and patiently answered our many requests for further information about their wines.

• Jean Smullen and the Wine Development Board of Ireland for so kindly allowing us the use of their tasting room.

• Aidan and Jimmy Redmond of Redmond's of Ranelagh for allowing us to disrupt their elegant wine shop for an entire morning while we arranged and rearranged bottles for the cover photograph.

Foreword

I have been in and around the wine arena, tasting, talking and writing, since 1959. Almost every imaginable challenge has been mine, including obituaries and appreciations. I have never written a foreword. It was worth waiting for; affording me a public platform to express feelings which would not fit comfortably elsewhere.

When I first primed my pen for *The Irish Times* there were only five regular wine columnists, to my knowledge, in the British Isles. Today there are at least 150 pen 'n' palates at work *pro bono publico*. This reflects a huge change in attitude at both trade and consumer level as wine enters the mass consumer market.

For the modern consumer knowledge and consciousness are akin to one another and for this reason information is sought and devoured. In this context, there is an increasingly healthy relationship between the trade and competent communicators. In fact, they both need each other. That the trade should trust Jacinta and her panel to objectively assess their wines is a fine compliment to the author.

I believe the challenge for our ilk is to take the intimidation out of wine buying and encourage all to explore the kaleidoscopic world of wine. Research has killed the myth of the super palate. Most are born with the same capacity to taste and smell.

The idea of wine experts bristling with sensory antennae and receiving mystical vibrations from every glass is plainly absurd. Professional judgements mostly reflect an intuition born out of years of practical experience. After three decades on the circuit I am conscious of the fallibility of decisions and the total uncertainty of all human predictions with regard to wine. However, experience does fine-tune judgement.

The path to connoisseurship is a different matter. It calls for experimentation, honesty, and the continued questioning of assumptions, and rejects the hypocrisy of label drinking. The latter begets excited expressions of appreciation for things fashionable whether they are enjoyed or not.

Scientists believe that we all live in our own 'taste world', so the route is different and very personal for all. There is no best wine, only the wine you like best at a price you can afford. Tastes evolve too. The challenge of exploration is invariably rewarded by the joy of discovery.

So use this publication as a friendly guide rather than as a bible. Do not look on the numbers or ratings as more than one person's judgement. Similar UK publications rate many of the wines quite differently. To quote the author, 'You may agree or disagree with some of our choices and results and we hope you do—after all, wine is about personal preference!'

In essence this book signposts the highways and byways for those who would like to explore their own sense of taste. Good taste is surely the hall-mark of culture and of a civilised lifestyle, whether it be applied to one's conversation, behaviour, dress, food or drink. It has nothing to do with wealth or fashion.

All pleasure—indeed all knowledge—comes to us through our senses. The latter have two purposes; to serve body and soul. In other words, they have a practical and an artistic dimension. The animal kingdom has developed far keener senses than ours but their usage is entirely utilitarian. They are merely for their survival through attack, defence and location of food for themselves and their young. A bird of prey would happily swap a Renoir or a Mouton Rothschild '45 for one plump pigeon. This is a measure of the difference between man and the animal kingdom.

Finally, I lift my glass to Jacinta, her panel and to a new generation of professionals as wine enters a golden era, enriching the lives of ever more Irish consumers. As with artists, musicians, chefs, *et al.*, it is not just love, instinct or experience but honesty, humility, and passion above all, which beget stars.

T. P. Whelehan

Introduction

Wine consumption in Ireland has doubled in the last fifteen years. We now drink just under eight bottles per head per year—in 1980 it was only four bottles and in 1960 just one bottle. Word in the trade is that the Irish consumer is open and adventurous, prepared to try unfamiliar wines, even those with totally baffling labels! The range on offer through supermarkets, off licences and specialist wine shops is wide and varied and developing all the time.

This wonderful variety has made the task of choosing wine much more exciting and rewarding, but also more confusing. Faced with rows of gleaming bottles, often with awkward names, the consumer too often finds him or herself leaving the shop with the old familiar. 'Keep ahold of nurse, for fear of finding something worse,' as the rhyme has it.

This guide is for those who wish to venture beyond nurse's protection but find that other wine guides do not relate to the Irish market. With so much being produced and available at all quality and price levels, in this case a little knowledge is a very good thing. This book reports the results of tasting over 1,100 wines from various regions, in price ranges from under £4 to over £100 a bottle. *All the wines are available in the Irish market at the time of publication.* The wines were supplied by importers. However, not all the wines we tasted have been included; so you can be sure those that are represent good quality.

To help you distinguish more precisely between wines, we have scored each one out of 20. The average score achieved by the selected wines is just over 13—the top score given, 17, is achieved by less than a dozen of the most superb wines. The character of each wine is described in a short tasting note written by Jacinta Delahaye.

The wines we have included all fulfilled the basic requirements of being well made at a reasonable price for their category. A number of the wines submitted for tasting were rejected, either because they did not meet our quality standards or the particular sample was in poor condition or past its peak. Since this is a current guide, we have concentrated on wines that are to be drunk now—some can be profitably laid down, but the tasting notes assumed current consumption. Indeed, many wines in today's market should be drunk young while fresh and fruity. This applies as much to red as to white wine. Ageing certainly will not improve them—quite the contrary. Different countries also like differing stages of maturity in their wine. The French drink their claret young, while the Irish prefer it more mature.

Styles such as basic Beaujolais and Beaujolais Nouveau, basic Côtes du Rhône and major brands (such as Piat d'Or or Jacob's Creek) are therefore produced to be bought quickly and drunk immediately. Other styles such as Rioja Reserva and Gran Reserva quality have done all their ageing in cask and bottle and are therefore ready to drink when released from the winery. We made our judgements on the vintages submitted.

What we found

White wines

There is much less 'bad' wine on the market than there used to be—in other words wines are technically better made. Inexpensive whites are usually fault free, but they can be very boring. The mid-price category offers more structure and flavour.

Varietal wines such as Sauvignon Blanc and Chardonnay (which should be instantly recognisable as being made from the particular grape) do not always live up to taste expectations. Styles can differ greatly.

Over-oaked whites tire the palate very quickly. More subtle use of oak adds greater interest to the final style of wine, particularly when Chardonnay-based.

Classic German Riesling can make memorable drinking.

South African Chenin (Steen) offers good food wines at reasonable prices.

Red wines

Corked wine is still a problem—we had to reject a number of samples offered. Reds are becoming less tannic and more fruity in style. Inexpensive reds are becoming more approachable (easy drinking). Easier-drinking reds are better served cool to highlight the fruit.

South African wines are making a big impact. Exciting regional styles are emerging from Australia. Pinotage is the red varietal to watch out for.

Merlot is producing super wines outside France. Check out Italy, Spain and Chile for top examples.

Italy is offering wonderful diversity in red wines. More and more good-value wines are coming from the South of France, Portugal, Eastern Europe and parts of Spain. Some very interesting sparkling wines are appearing on the market at very good value. Don't forget the great pleasure to be had from fortified and dessert wines.

Finally, you may agree or disagree with some of our choices and results and, in a sense, we hope you do—after all, wine is all about personal preference!

How to Use This Guide

Each wine is listed first of all under its country of origin (and region in the case of France), then by colour and price band, and finally in alphabetical order by the name of the wine.

As well as a tasting note describing the kind of wine you can expect, each wine is given a score out of twenty (see below for more detail on the scoring system). The tasting notes indicate the style of wine; how these were written is described in more detail below.

Most wines included in the guide are widely available throughout the country in supermarkets, off licences and/or wine merchants. The importer's name is given (in brackets); if you wish to find your nearest outlet for a particular wine, contact the importer, who will be happy to advise you.

Some wines are available only through off licences specialising in wine or through wine merchants; this is indicated by the words *Wine merchants/off licences*. Again, in case of difficulty contact the importer for your nearest outlet. Entries for wines stocked exclusively by one outlet, or only available direct from the importer, include only the outlet/importer's name in italics: for example, *Dunnes Stores* or *Wines Direct*.

See pages 254–6 for a list of importers included in this guide with their addresses and telephone numbers.

See pages 257–64 for a selected list of retail outlets specialising in wine.

The Tastings

Each of the wines was tasted and scored. *Jacinta Delahaye* chaired the panel and tasted all the wines. All the tasting notes were written by her, based on the discussions of the panel. The scores were averaged from those assigned by the members. The unsigned introductory articles were also written by her; the signed articles were written by members of the tasting panel.

Jacinta Delahaye is a wine consultant, educator and writer. She holds the Wine and Spirit Education Trust Diploma and has been working in the wine trade in Ireland for over ten years. Her consultancy clients include Dunnes Stores, the Shelbourne Hotel, and Food and Wine from France. She is Wine and Spirits Editor of *Shelf Life* and co-author, with Sandy O'Byrne, of *Wining and Dining at Home in Ireland*.

The panel/contributors

Didier Fiat, Head Sommelier at the Kildare Hotel and Country Club, comes from a family of wine growers in Languedoc-Roussillon. He holds the Wine and Spirit Education Trust Diploma. In 1992 he won the Sopexa Best Irish Sommelier award, and was also awarded the title of World Best Sommelier, Bronze Medal, by ASI (Association de la Sommellerie Internationale).

Tom Franks, wine lecturer and correspondent, has spent over forty years in the wine trade. He was Chairman of the Wine Promotion Board of Ireland for five years.

Mary Gaynor lectures for the Wine Development Board of Ireland. She holds the Wine and Spirit Education Trust Diploma.

Catherine Griffith is a wine educator and has recently joined the Molloy Group as wine consultant. She holds the Wine and Spirit Education Trust Diploma.

Noel Kierans, Barrister-at-Law, is in the financial services field. He holds the Wine and Spirit Education Trust Diploma, winning the Grants of Ireland scholarship. He advises a number of establishments on their wine cellars.

Breda McSweeney, of Lacken House Restaurant, has won many national sommelier competitions and has represented Ireland in three world finals. She is a Commanderer in the Association Internationale des Maîtres Conseils en Gastronomie Française.

Monica Murphy of the Cheeseboard Ltd, Dublin, is a professional wine and cheese consultant, lecturer and writer who travels extensively to vineyard areas as a guide for consumer and trade wine tours. She holds the Wine and Spirit Education Trust Diploma.

Aideen Nolan joined the Wine Development Board of Ireland at its inception and was heavily involved in setting up educational courses for the trade and for consumers. She holds the Wine and Spirit Education Trust Diploma, and is currently studying to be a Master of Wine.

Dermot Nolan is an independent wine broker and consultant. He started studying wine in 1989, holds the Wine and Spirit Education Trust Diploma, and is currently studying to be a Master of Wine.

David Power worked in the wine trade in Ireland for over thirty years with Edward Dillon and Co. He is now an independent wine consultant and also lectures for the Wine Development Board of Ireland.

Other contributors

Sandy O'Byrne is a food, wine and travel writer. She is co-author, with Jacinta Delahaye, of *Wining and Dining at Home in Ireland*.

George O'Malley (1926–95) was Director of the Wine and Spirit Association of Ireland for many years and Director of the Wine Development Board of Ireland.

Some members of our panel act as advisers to particular wine importers. These members withdrew from the panel when the wines of the firm they advise were tasted.

Scores

Only wines which scored 11 or above were included in the guide. Wines were assessed within their price categories, so that scores reflect the panel's judgement of the wine's price/quality ratio. The average score (which of course does not include the wines we discarded) was just over 13. Star wines, that is those scoring 15, 16 or 17, are indicated with stars in the margin. Some 15 per cent received stars—only a tiny percentage received three stars (17 points).

What the scores indicate:

11 = basic well-made wine

12 = acceptable quality with good flavour

13 = good quality in its price/style category

14 = very good quality

15 = excellent quality and worthy of attention— indicated by one star

16 = top quality—indicated by two stars

17 = superb quality and very difficult to fault—indicated by three stars

There is no ideal way to rate a wine: wine-drinking is a pleasure, and its appreciation is an art; as with painting, poetry or music, personal preferences are part of the enjoyment; today we feel like listening to Mozart, tomorrow the Cranberries; so it is with wine; a fine Châteauneuf-du-Pape will match one mood, a Fleurie another. A numerical rating is useful, however, when trying to pick out exceptional wines, or to convey our panel's view of a straightforward, perfectly acceptable, but not outstanding wine.

Prices

Wine prices are not fixed. Different retailers may raise or lower the price of individual wines as they choose. On the other hand, we felt it desirable to indicate the approximate price. All the wines are therefore listed in order of price band. The following bands were chosen:

Up to £4.50	£4.50 to £5.25
£5.25 to £6.50	£6.50 to £8
£8 to £10	£10 to £12
£12 to £15	£15 to £20
£20 to £30	£30 to £50
£50 to £100	Over £100

(Since these are indication bands, not exact divisions, we have avoided the statistical nicety of bands beginning £6.51, £8.01 etc.)

We have made every effort to assign wines to their appropriate price bands, but please remember that these are guide prices only: prices may vary from one outlet to another, because of promotions, for example, or bulk buying; they may change because of fluctuations in exchange rates, changes in taxes and excise, and so on.

In the price bands up to £5.25 we looked for well-made wines with some flavour; from £5.25 to £6.50 fruity flavours. Between £6.50 and £10 we wanted more structure, and between £10 and £15 structure, flavour and balance. Beyond £15 we increasingly sought complexity and ageing ability.

The £6.50–£10 price categories proved the most exciting. The word from the trade is that Irish consumers, unlike their British counterparts, are willing to trade up from low prices if the quality demands. For unforgettable wines you still have to pay from £12 upwards.

Some Important Grape Varieties

Increasingly wines are described on their labels by the variety of grape that went into their production. This is known as varietal labelling. Listed below are some of the more important of the literally hundreds of varieties of grape cultivated across the world.

White grape varieties

Chardonnay: Native of Burgundy, it has now spread across the world. It has great affinity with oak. Flavours and aromas range from wet wool to apple in unoaked styles to melon, vanilla, butter and toast with oak influence.

Chenin Blanc: Also known as Steen in South Africa, famed in the Loire for producing styles of white wine ranging from dry to sweet, some of which have great ability to age. All are marked by high acidity. Flavours are marzipan, ripe red apples and honey. Fruity styles are produced in South Africa.

Gewürztraminer: Important in Alsace and German wines, this grape produces wines with low acidity, high alcohol and scents of roses and Turkish delight.

Muscat: The most 'grapey' of varieties, producing a wide span of styles of wines, from dry to sweet, and from sparkling to fortified. A heavily scented grape. Flavours range from orange peel and marmalade to prunes and raisins.

Riesling: One of the world's great white grapes. Wines produced from it are always marked by a lively acidity and good fruit. At its very best in Germany and Alsace, it is also an important variety in Australia. Granny Smith apples, petrol and orange blossom describe some of the aromas of wines produced from this grape.

Sauvignon Blanc: At its best in the Loire and New Zealand. In California it is aged in oak and known as Fumé Blanc. Definite rhubarb tones are recognisable in this style.

Without oak, the grape delivers aromas and tastes of gooseberry, nettles, elderflower, runner beans and asparagus.

Sémillon: At its very best in the Hunter Valley of Australia and the Sauternes district of Bordeaux. It has a very herbaceous grassy tone when vinified as a dry wine. In the Hunter Valley it has great ageing ability and wines that start dry assume honey nuances with age. In Bordeaux it contributes to the blend of dry white wines. When affected by noble rot it also produces some of the world's greatest sweet wines—Sauternes being a top example.

Viognier: A fashionable grape of the 1990s. Viognier is a delicate and difficult grape to grow, doing best in the northern Rhône. Reminiscent of peaches and apricots.

Red grape varieties

Cabernet Sauvignon: This thick-skinned grape produces darkly coloured tannic wines noted for their ageing potential. It also has a great affinity with oak. Flavours range from thin and weedy when it is grown in too cold a climate to jammy and blowsy when it is too hot. Under the right conditions it produces some of the best red wines in the world. Always used as part of a blend in classic wines such as Bordeaux and top estate wines from South Africa. Also used as a varietal in most other regions.

Merlot: Famous for their deep colour, wines produced from this grape are earlier maturing than their Cabernet Sauvignon counterparts. At its most majestic in St Emilion and Pomerol in Bordeaux. Bulgaria, north-east Italy, Chile and California are all producing good Merlot wines. Flavours range from fruit cake to woodland undergrowth.

Syrah: Syrah is known as Shiraz in Australia. Marked with lots of spicy tones the grape gives good colour. As well as fruit, Syrah can also impart pepper, spice and minty tones. Hermitage from the Rhône is a top example of Syrah. Try an Australian to compare the difference in style.

Pinot Noir: Difficult to grow, the grape gives medium colour. At its supreme best in Burgundy, producing complex wines with a characteristic 'farmyard' aroma. Washington State and the cooler parts of Australia and California are also producing some very good examples of this tantalising grape.

Nebbiolo: Grown in Italy. Small with a thick skin, the grapes are dark in colour and produce tannic acid wine with great ageing ability, especially in Piedmont in north Italy. Comparisons with liquorice, prunes and figs are often used to describe the flavour.

Sangiovese: Grown in Italy. Can be very light bodied or full and round. Has a tendency to lose its colour quickly. Most important in the production of Chianti, the grape imparts flavours of cherry and spice.

Tempranillo: Best known for producing Rioja and easy-drinking fruity wines. With oak, particularly American oak, influence it assumes more rounded tones. Strawberry and coconut flavours.

Zinfandel: Native to California. Produces styles of wine ranging from jammy to rich and spicy. Used extensively for the production of blush (rosé) wine. Blackberry jam is a good term to describe the flavour.

Grape growing in Ireland

Grapes are extremely difficult to grow successfully in our cold damp climate. Wines produced here tend to be fruity in style with high acidity. Production is very small.

Blackwater Valley: Located in Mallow, Co. Cork and owned by Dr William Christopher. Reichensteiner, Seyval Blanc and Madeleine Angevine are the principal vines.

Longueville House: Located in Mallow, Co. Cork, and owned by Michael O'Callaghan who is proud to serve his white wine in his restaurant.

West Waterford Vineyard: Located at Affane near Cappoquin and owned by Patricia and David McGrath. Wine is sold from the vineyard itself.

Buying, Storing, Serving and Tasting Wine

Buying wine

It all starts in the off-licence or supermarket where bottles of wine stand upright, in line, ready to be picked. Because this is a small country, and turnover in stock may sometimes be slow, some wines may remain on the shelves, unsold, for weeks or even months. The bottles in the front may become oxidised under the shop's fluorescent light. Still and sparkling white wines are the most susceptible to light spoilage. I usually pick the bottle at the back, just to be on the safe side.

It is wrong to think that all wines improve with time. Vin de pays, rosé and most other wines that retail for under £6 are made for immediate consumption—they are not meant to be stored. More expensive wines such as non-vintage still, sparkling or dessert styles will keep for a few months but their aromas and flavours will begin to fade after that. However, there are some exceptions to the general rule that only the most expensive wines have the ability to improve with time. If we are patient enough, some lower-priced wines can be very rewarding indeed. For example, store half a dozen or more of the Beaujolais cru, Moulin à Vent, for at least six or seven years. The wine in time will totally lose its initial Beaujolais profile to become almost Burgundian in style with an unusual finesse. Another notable exception is red Melnik from Bulgaria: for less than £6 it has remarkable keeping qualities.

Storing wine

Wine will mature only under the best storage conditions. At 12°C, maturation is normal. At 16–18°C, maturation accelerates and at 20°C and over wines will deteriorate in the long term. Frequent temperature variations, which will not affect the wine in the short term, should be avoided during long-term storage. Make sure the room or cellar where the wines are stored has a good humidity level—70 per cent is best. This will ensure that the corks remain moist and do not shrink, which could allow air to enter, leading to oxidation. It is important to lay bottles on their sides to keep the part of the cork in contact with the wine moist as well.

Remember that corks absorb strong odours and transfer them to wine in the long run. Therefore avoid storing items such as oil-based paints, fuel or vegetables like leeks and onions in the same room as your wine. Finally, if you are in a hurry, it might be useful to know that half-bottles age faster due to their higher air to wine ratio. If you are storing your wine for posterity, remember that magnums will mature at a much slower pace.

Serving wine

The enjoyment of wine is enhanced by serving it at the right temperature. Far too often white wines are served too cold and red wines too warm. White and rosé wines are meant to be drunk cool to cold according to preference, but never too cold, as this will detract from the wine's aroma and flavour. Dry white and rosé wines should be drunk cool, at around 10°C to maximise aroma and flavour. Young red wines with low tannin—for example red Vin de Pays, Beaujolais Nouveau, Bag-in-box or Valpolicella— are better served rather cool, to enhance their fruity character. Serve them between 12°C and 15°C. The 'bigger' styles, like Châteauneuf-du-Pape, Barolo or Bordeaux cru classé, are best served between 16°C and 18°C. Below 16°C the tannins could appear excessive and above 18°C these could become slightly heady (especially over 20°C) and lose balance.

How to taste wine

The first step to take, so that wine tasting becomes truly relevant and fascinating, is to go beyond terms such as 'nice', 'lovely' or 'beautiful' when trying to describe wine. These words convey a general sense of quality but do not give proportion and measure to the sensation received.

An 'intensely floral' yet 'delicate' Riesling from Germany, a 'slender', 'elegant' Bordeaux or a 'rich', 'opulent' Château Musar from Lebanon would be more appropriate tasting terms to describe these wines.

The appearance of a wine tells us about its state of maturity. Red wines have a deep, blueish-purple rim when one to two years old, changing to ruby and mahogany, almost orange, when fully mature at fifteen to twenty years and over. Needless to say we should not wait for a lively Beaujolais Nouveau to fade this far just for the sake of the colour!

White wines display a huge palette of different shades from water white or pale lemon with hints of green to 24 carat gold.

A myriad of scents can be discovered in a glass of wine. At least 650 known constituents have been isolated in wine so far, many having direct or indirect effects on the bouquet. So why worry if our friend gets blackcurrant in his or her glass of Cabernet Sauvignon and we get green pepper? Both parties would be correct. Technically, gas chromatography has always demonstrated a dominance of these two aromatic compounds in Cabernets.

What is more revealing (and what no instrument can read) is our ability to discern the character of aromas on the nose. Is it bland, neutral, unripe, ripe, overripe, withered, fresh, complex, youthful, mature?

On the palate, check if the intensity of flavour mounts to a crescendo. This is a sure sign of high quality. Is the fruit sweet, or savoury? New World wines tend to be overtly fruity, whereas traditional western European wines can be more restrained and austere in style.

The feel of the wine—its structure and texture—is very

important. Is it soft, firm, lean, round, full-bodied, massive? Is its texture silky, astringent, creamy, chewy, juicy? Try, for example, a good Merlot (or St Émilion) from any country and compare it to a Cabernet Sauvignon (or Médoc) from the same country at around the same price. Appreciate the generous character, the rotund shape and smooth touch of the Merlot. Cabernet is leaner and, despite its high fruit extracts, has a tougher profile due to its high tannin content combined with unusually good acidity.

Finally, to assess quality in a wine, simply consider how well intensity and finesse mingle together, how deep and full flavoured it is, but above all how memorable. Surely this should lead us to understand that the whole point of wine appreciation is knowing how to taste the difference when we are prepared to pay the difference.

Happy tasting!

Didier Fiat

	69	70	71	72	73	74	75	76	77	78	79	80	81	82	83
Bordeaux—white	●●	●●●	●●●	●	●●●	●●	●●●	●●●	●●	●●●	●●●	●●	●●●	●●	●●●
Médoc-Graves	●	★	●●	●	●●	●●	★	★★★★	●●	★★	●●●	●●	●●●	★	●●●
St Emilion Pomerol	●	●●●	●●●	●●●	●●	●	●●	●●	●●	★	●●●	●●	●●●	★★	●●●
Burgundy—white	●●●	●●●	●●●	●●●	●●●	●●	●●	●●	●	●●●	●●●	●●	●●●	●●●	●●●
Burgundy—red	★	●●	●●●	●●●	●	●	●●	●●	●	●●●	●●●	●●	●●●	●●●	★
Northern Rhône	●●●	★	●●	●●	●●	●	★★	★★★★	●	★	●●●	●●	●●	●●●	●
Southern Rhône	●●●	●●●	●●●	●●	●	●	●	●●	●	●	●●●	●●	●●	●●●	●
Alsace	●●●	●●●	★	●●●	●●	●	★★	●●	●	●●	●●●	●●	●●●	●●●	●
Loire	●●●	●●●	★★★	●●	●	●	★★	●●	●	★	●●●	●●●	●●●	★	★
Germany—Mosel	●●●	●●●	●●●	●●	●●	●	●●●	●●	●	●●●	●●●	●	●●●	●●●	●●
Germany—Rhein	●●●	●●●	●●●	●●	●●	●	●●●	●●	●	●●●	●●●	●	●●●	★	●●
Italy—Piedmont	●●	★	★	●●	●●	●	●●	●	●	★★	●●●	●●	●●●	★	★
Italy—Tuscany	●●	●●	●●	●	●●	●●	●●	●	●●	●●	●●	●●	●	●●	●●
Spain—Rioja	●●●	●	●●	●●	●●	★	●●●	●●	●	●●●	●●●	●●	●●●	●●	●●
California	●	●●	●●	●	●	★	●●	●●	●	●●	●●	●●	●	●●	●
Sauternes	●	★	●●	●●	●●	●	●●●	●●●	●	●●●	●●●	●●	●●	●●	★
Port (vintage)	—	★	—	●●	—	—	●●	—	★	●●	—	●●	—	●●	●●

	84	85	86	87	88	89	90	91	92	93	94
Bordeaux—white	•••	•••	•••	••	•••	★	★	••	••	•••	•••
Médoc-Graves	••	•••	•••	••	•••	★	★	•	••	•••	••
St Emilion Pomerol	•	•••	•••	••	•••	★	★	•	••	•••	•••
Burgundy—white	•••	•••	•••	••	•••	★	•••	••	•••	•	••
Burgundy—red	••	★	★	••	★	•••	★	••	••	•••	•
Northern Rhône	•••	★	••	••	•••	•••	★	••	••	••	•••
Southern Rhône	•••	••	••	••	•••	★	★	••	••	••	•••
Alsace	••	••	••	••	•••	★	★	••	••	••	•••
Loire	•	★	••	••	•••	★	★	••	••	••	•••
Germany—Mosel	••	•••	•••	••	•••	•••	★	•••	••	••	•••
Germany—Rhein	•••	•••	•••	••	•••	•••	★	•••	•••	••	•••
Italy—Piedmont	••	★	•••	••	•••	★	•••	••	•	••	•••
Italy—Tuscany	••	★	••	••	★	••	••	••	••	••	•••
Spain—Rioja	•••	★	•••	•••	★	★	★	••	••	••	★
California	•	★	••	★	★	••	••	★	•••	••	••
Sauternes	••	•••	•••	•	•	—	•••	•	•	•	••
Port (vintage)	—	•••	—	—	—	—	••	★	★	••	★

Wine and Food

Wine and food are natural partners. Most wine is drunk with food and in most traditional wine regions the cuisine has evolved to match the local wine. Yet in spite of an almost instinctive association, the combination varies from entirely casual on the one hand to over-elaboration on the other. It is in fact common sense. In France, wine has long been called the 'second sauce' and, just as orange sauce is an unlikely accompaniment to the finest Aberdeen Angus, a light, fruity, lively wine is similarly inappropriate. This is not so much a matter of rules as of principles of taste, and to break them without reason or simply for the sake of it won't do justice to either the food or the wine.

Getting the taste right has limitations. The sense of taste is perhaps the most subjective of all the senses; it is influenced also by mood, environment and company. As wine and food are both natural products (or at least should be), they are far from consistent; the same wine or the same dish will rarely taste the same twice.

That regional combinations of wine and food are successful is the first clue to understanding the nature of this particular kind of compatibility. In vine-growing areas of France, Italy, Spain and indeed much of Europe, surprising examples of the perfect match are constantly found. The strange, slightly oily white wines of Cassis in the South of France come into their own with local fish stews; olive-oil-bathed sardines are perfect with dry, woody Portuguese reds, while the much maligned Lambrusco is the only accompaniment to the impossibly rich *zampone* of its north Italian home.

In traditional regions the wine blends not just with a type of food, but with a method of cooking and particular flavours like garlic, herbs and olive oil. This must be remembered in matching wine and food from other areas—it is the whole dish with its flavourings, sauces and garnishes that must combine with the wine, not just the principal ingredient. For example, a pan-fried chicken breast with a lemon and parsley butter will go well with a light dry white wine such as a Frascati. If it had a sauce of wild mushrooms, wine and cream, a medium-bodied red such as Chianti would be more appropriate, while an exotic stir-fried chicken would need an equally spicy wine like Gewürztraminer from Alsace. When you consider a specific wine for a specific dish the possibilities become endless.

But just as wines may be divided broadly into categories of light, medium, aromatic and full-bodied, so dishes can be considered in different styles. A dish may be mild or strong, meaty or delicate, simple or complex. The texture is just as important as the taste and is the first thing to consider when choosing the wine. A delicate fish like plaice served with a simple butter sauce would be overpowered by a full-bodied, oak-influenced Burgundy with its layers of taste. It needs a wine that is light, simple and with enough acidity to cut the butter and bring out the taste of the fish, for example a Muscadet. On the other hand, a fine slice of turbot with a shellfish sauce would completely lose the Muscadet but be greatly enhanced by a Meursault. In both these examples it is the weight and texture of the dish as much as the flavour that influences the choice of wine.

There are a number of problematic ingredients that may make wine choice difficult. Acidic foods such as citrus fruit or its juice, tomatoes, vinaigrette sauce, etc. are hard on wines as they increase the impact of the wine's own acidity. A really sharp dish will damage any wine, but for foods with moderate acidity like tomatoes, wines that combine acidity with fruit can work well. Beaujolais with tomato sauce or New Zealand Sauvignon Blanc with prawns and lemon grass are examples of wines whose own considerable acidity is masked by lots of fruit.

Egg dishes, including sauces and mayonnaise and very rich creamy foods, have the opposite problem of being too alkaline, of simply dulling the taste of wine. The answer is a wine with body from either alcohol and extract or sweetness which will counteract the richness and low acidity of the food. Sauternes with foie gras is an obvious, somewhat extreme example. Spices are also difficult. Very hot chillis are impossible; leave it to lager, or water. Gentler, aromatic spices can work well with flavoursome white wines, while Chinese flavours go with fruity or floral wine notes.

Tannic reds will positively clash with spicy foods as both are bitter flavours and taste harsh together.

The texture and any difficult flavours establish the kind of wine best suited to a particular dish. After that come individual flavours. Fundamentally, the stronger the flavours in the dish—the more garlic and herbs, the use of a sauce or marinade and the number of different flavours it combines—the more primary flavours are needed from the wine. Primary flavours are fruit, varietal character and oak tastes. A more subtle dish, in which all the ingredients are blended together in a more harmonious taste, will benefit from and enhance a complex wine. For example, a leg of lamb cooked with lots of garlic and rosemary needs a vigorous young Bordeaux redolent of blackcurrants and spicy oak. A rack of lamb with a simple *jus* enriched with wine would be the perfect foil for an older, more fragile Bordeaux, whose complex flavours would be brought out by the simple, refined nature of the food. Remember there is only so much the palate can take on board: great complexity in the glass and on the plate are too much to appreciate.

Two sweet tastes are generally considered to be more difficult to match than two savoury ones. The reason for this is that fine dessert wine is naturally sweet, its lusciousness coming from super-ripe fruit and concentrated natural sugars. Many desserts, cakes and pastries are based on pure sugar, which is much 'sweeter' and more cloying. The natural sweetness of the wine simply cannot match this.

Perfectly ripe fruit, simple fruit tarts or peaches and

apricots, nutty cakes and certain hot soufflés are excellent foods for dessert wines.

Wine and flavour checklist

Dominant flavour	*Type of wine*
Salty	Clean, refreshing styles e.g. sparkling wine, Italian white wines, unoaked Merlot
Tart, citrusy or sharp (if excessive will clash with wine)	Acidity cloaked with fruit e.g. New Zealand Sauvignon, Beaujolais
Hot (not suitable for wine if very hot)	Aromatic and fruity wines, avoid tannin e.g. Fumé Blanc, Spätlese Riesling, rosé, lighter Côtes du Rhône and Corbières
Earthy (mushrooms, reduction sauces)	Strong, full-bodied dry whites, mature reds e.g. Chablis, Reserva Rioja, Riserva Chianti, Pinot Noir
Smoky (smoked fish, meat, aubergines)	Aromatic and oaky whites, fruity and spicy reds e.g. Sauvignon Blanc, Pinot Gris (Grigio), North Italian reds, Rhône reds, Médoc reds
Sweet (spice such as cinnamon and nutmeg, Chinese food, mint, fennel, sweet peppers, cooked garlic and onions)	Medium- to full-bodied whites with balanced acidity, medium-bodied reds with soft to balanced tannin e.g. Sémillon, oaked

	Chardonnay, white Graves, Alsace whites, New World Cabernet Sauvignon and some Shiraz
Herbal	Aromatic whites, dry medium-bodied reds e.g. Sauvignon Blanc, Verdicchio, Languedoc-Roussillon and Provence reds, St Emilion, Californian Cabernet Sauvignon

Sandy O'Byrne

THE WINES

d'Arenberg *Mc Laren Vale* *Australia*	**Santa Julia** *Mendoza* *Argentina*
Santa Helena *Curico Valley* *Chile*	**Carpineto** *Tuscany* *Italy*
Robert Sarrau *Beaujolais & Crus* *France*	**Malesan** *Bordeaux* *France*
Ch Lagrange **Ch Logis de Sipian** **Ch Pichon**	**Achaia Claus** *Patras* *Greece*

For name of your local retailer contact -

Taserra Wine Merchants

Shippers of Fine Wines & Spirits since 1976
Hogan House, Grand Canal St., Dublin 2
Ph 4900537   Fax 490 4052

Importers of - Muscadet, Sancerre, Chablis, Pommard, Aloxe Corto
St Aubin, Nuits St Georges, Mersault, Medoc, St Julien, St Emilion
Graves, Chateauneuf du Pape, Cotes du Rhone and wines from
Germany, Spain, Switzerland, South Africa, Portugal, Algeria etc.

Argentina

Argentina is one of the main producers of wine in South America. Unlike Chile, Argentina is not entirely phylloxera free, but the louse cannot thrive due to the high sand content in its soil. Lack of humidity reduces the risk of fungal disease, so the cost of spraying crops is greatly reduced. In 1990 modern viticulture practices and improved technology in wineries were introduced.

The main area of production is Cuyo, which comprises two provinces, Mendoza, which is on the other side of the mountains from Santiago, and San Juan, a little further north. Grapes are grown on smallholdings, and are sold under contract to private bodegas or co-operatives.

Argentina is a good source of inexpensive but well-made red wines of deep colour. Malbec is the most important grape variety, producing rich, vigorous, fruity red oak-aged wines of good structure. The Malbec, which is grown on the less fertile hills, often achieves better results in Mendoza than in its native South-West France. Pinot Noir and Cabernet Sauvignon wines are increasing, while Italian influence accounts for some Sangiovese and Barbera.

Some white wine is produced, including Chardonnay, Chenin Blanc and Riesling. The main producers are Santa Ana, and Penaflor, who own Trapiche, which is a prestigious quality bodega and leads the modern movement. Orfila is noted for crisp white wines. The quality of white wines continues to improve, due to better location of vineyards at higher altitudes, early picking of grapes to retain acid, and temperature-controlled fermentation, producing pale golden fresh wines with a touch of spice.

Argentinian wines represented in Ireland include Trapiche, Etchart, Luigi Bosca and Santa Julia.

Breda McSweeney

WHITE WINES

Whites under £5.25

Etchart Cafayate Torrontes 93   13
(Fitzgeralds)   *Wine merchants/off licences*
Good quality/price ratio. Intense floral and Muscat
aromas and lime freshness on the finish.

Whites between £5.25 and £6.50

Etchart Cafayate Chardonnay 93   11
(Fitzgeralds)   *Wine merchants/off licences*
Fruity, with hints of peach and apricot. Dry finish.

Santa Julia nv   11
(Taserra)   *Widely available*
Crisp and clean with emphasis on fruit. Off-dry.

Santa Julia, Torrontes Riojano 95   13
(Taserra)   *Widely available*
Named after the grape variety which is unique to
Argentina. Light colour. Aromatic ripe fruit and floral
tone reminiscent of the Muscat grape. Good acidity and
alcohol levels with a fruity finish.

Santa Julia Chardonnay 94   13
(Taserra)   *Widely available*
Fat and rich with tropical fruit tones ending in a hint of
coconut and cut through with refreshing acidity.

Trapiche Chardonnay Oak Cask 92   14
(United Beverages)   *Widely available*
The buttery aspect to the background of ripe melon fruit
is very appealing. Well balanced with a long finish.

White between £10 and £12

Navarro Correas Chardonnay 94   14
(Greenhills)   *Wine merchants/off licences*
An elegant grand style of Chardonnay. Buttery-creamy
tones, good fruit and lemony acidity.

RED WINES

Reds under £5.25

Etchart Mendoza 93   12
(Fitzgeralds)   *Wine merchants/off licences*
Dense smoky aromas. Slightly opaque in colour with a
good attack of red berry fruits with a soft centre and
good finish. Serve cool to enhance fruit.

Trapiche Cabernet Sauvignon Reserve 90   14
(United Beverages)   *Widely available*
Good tangy bite of fruit with enough acidity and tannin
to give grip and length on the finish.

Reds between £5.25 and £6.50

Etchart Cabernet Sauvignon 91   13
(Fitzgeralds)   *Widely available*
Wonderful deep garnet saturation with definite pea-pod
aromas. Lots of ripe fruit impact which evolves and
continues right through to the long lovely finish.

Etchart Lujan de Cuyo Malbec 93   12
(Fitzgeralds)   *Wine merchants/off licences*
Packed with loganberry fruits and ending in a long
finish.

Santa Julia Malbec 93   12
(Taserra)   *Widely available*
Wines made from Malbec can be quite tannic, tight and
closed when young. With bottle age they develop
softness with rounded-out ripe red berry fruits and a
touch of spice. This is a good example.

Santa Julia Mendoza Cabernet Sauvignon 93   12
(Taserra)   *Widely available*
Closed dumb nose, but plenty of fruits waiting to
emerge. Good structure with drying tannins and good
acidity balance.

Trapiche Cabernet Sauvignon Oak Cask 86   14
  (United Beverages)   *Widely available*
Wonderful deep ruby colour. Broad ripe fruit tones
wrap around vanilla oak to give good length to the
finish.

Trapiche Malbec Oak Cask 88   14
  (United Beverages)   *Widely available*
Good attack of ripe fruits with a slight stalkiness coming
through. Nice creamy touch to the finish.

Red between £8 and £10

★**Arnaldo B. Etchart 90**   15
  (Fitzgeralds)   *Widely available*
An intensely focused wine. Bitter chocolate attack
overlain with smoky tones and enough tannin to ensure
further maturation.

Reds between £10 and £12

★★**Bosca Malbec 91**   16
  (Greenhills)   *Wine merchants/off licences*
A marvellous combination of ripe, red berry fruits with
hints of spice make this a classic. Elegant finish.

★★**Bosca Syrah 88**   16
  (Greenhills)   *Wine merchants/off licences*
Superbly balanced with intense fruit cut through with a
spicy finish. A clear favourite with the panel.

★★**Navarro Correas Cabernet Sauvignon 88**   16
  (Greenhills)   *Wine merchants/off licences*
Superb drinking. 80% Cabernet Sauvignon and 20%
Merlot, with a good balance of fruit and tannin. Pre-
sented in a frosted bottle.

Australia

Australia's wine industry began over two hundred years ago in Sydney, New South Wales. The first vines arrived with the early settlers in 1788 and probably came from the Cape of Good Hope, which had been colonised by the Dutch and was the last port of call for ships to stock up with water before sailing on to Australia.

Life was hard. Free settlers eventually moved further away from the large cities, clearing land for farming and planting vineyards. Vine-growing and winemaking were very much influenced by the skills brought with them from their native countries.

In the 1830s James Busby, a Scotsman known as the father of the Australian wine industry, was given a grant by the British Government to plant a large vineyard holding in the Hunter Valley. An acknowledged expert in his own day, he spent a lot of time in European wine regions and brought many vine varieties with him to Australia. During his voyage to the continent he wrote a treatise on 'The Culture of the Vine and the Art of Winemaking'.

Progress continued unabated until about 1870, when the scourge phylloxera attacked the vineyards of Australia. The First and Second World Wars also saw a halt to the development of the wine industry.

In the 1950s the home market taste was for strong fortified wines, big blowsy reds and oxidised whites. Things began to change dramatically in the 1960s, which saw the emergence of drier table wines. Improved technology such as cold fermentation and temperature control, plus the rediscovery of old pre-phylloxera areas and a general increase in the consumption of table wines meant a huge resurgence for the whole industry.

The mid-1970s and 1980s saw great developments in the winery, with better use of technology, yeasts, oak, bottling, etc. Now there is a strong move towards the vineyard. New areas are being discovered, grape varieties are being selected to suit particular sites, and experimentation on irrigation, planting and pruning continues in the quest to achieve ever better-quality fruit.

Present day

Australia is the eleventh largest wine-producing country in the world with an average annual output of 12m gallons of wine. There are 802 wine producers in Australia, not necessarily in separate wineries. The industry is dominated by four big producers, the Southcorp Group, Orlando Wyndham, BRL Hardy and Mildara Blass. They are responsible for about 80 per cent of total Australian production. Medium-sized companies with big reputations include Yalumba, Rosemount and Brown Brothers. Other producers may rely on contract winemaking facilities, but typically have their own vineyards, cellar door sales and distinctive brands.

Styles of white wine

Chardonnay: Produces excellent flavoursome wines with exotic fruit aromas influenced by vanilla tones of oak. Different regional characteristics are evident in the pineapple tastes of Hunter Valley Chardonnay compared to the limey style of Padthaway and the rich concentrated styles of the Margaret River.

Chardonnay/Sémillon: Popular in Australia, this blend produces melon-type aromas and flavours and is usually competitively priced.

Sémillon: Depending on where it is produced, can vary in style from dry and herbaceous to full-bodied with oak influence. Often confused with Chardonnay. Some of the best come from the Hunter Valley and Western Australia, and are noted for their great ability to age, assuming honey tones when mature.

Sémillon/Sauvignon Blanc: Not often seen in Ireland, this blend offers an interesting combination. The silky weighty texture of Sémillon, with its ability to age, harmonises very well with the aromatic qualities of Sauvignon Blanc.

Rhine Riesling: This noble white grape variety has always been very popular in Australia. It varies in style from dry and light, to medium dry, to sweet and rich if affected by noble rot. The best come from the Clare Valley and the Eden Valley.

Muscat: Different styles are produced from different versions of this grape. Top quality comes from Muscat à Petits Grains. They range from the delicate, fresh, late-picked dessert wines to the glorious liqueur Muscats and Tokays.

Verdelho: Used in the production of Madeira. Produces notable zesty full-bodied table wines from Western Australia.

Styles of red wine

Shiraz: Australia's most widely planted red variety. Produces a myriad of styles, from easy drinking good-value wines to more complex, spicy, lush styles. Often blended with Cabernet Sauvignon to produce well-structured, rich, classy wines. Different wine-making techniques result in varying styles, but most wines have oak (American or French) influence.

Cabernet Sauvignon: No matter where it is produced, its character is blackcurrant fruitiness. Cabernet Sauvignon wines from Coonawarra, Victoria and Western Australia are complex and elegant, while those from the Barossa and Clare are noted for their up-front fruit flavours. Most are matured in French or American oak.

Merlot: Good examples made from Australian Merlot have instant appeal, producing opulent and succulent wines.

Pinot Noir: Not extensively planted, Australian Pinot Noir is all about strawberry/raspberry fruits. Main production areas include Victoria, Adelaide Hills, Yarra Valley and Tasmania. Often used in sparkling wine production.

Tarrango: Developed in Australia in 1965, it is a cross between the white Sultana and the red Portuguese Touriga. The variety produces fruity light red wines for early drinking and is at its best served cool.

Grenache: Extremely popular in Australia, it has a pronounced raspberry character with hints of cigar box.

Sparkling wine

Sparkling: Every third bottle of wine drunk in Australia is a 'fizzy' and recent years have seen investment by French Champagne houses such as Moët & Chandon, Roederer and Bollinger. Wines are produced by the traditional (Champagne) method or by the transfer method.

WHITE WINES

Whites under £4.50

Moyston Australian Riesling 93   14
                                        Dunnes Stores

Good quality/price ratio with clean fresh limey flavours and an off-dry finish.

Moyston Colombard/Chardonnay 93   13
                                        Dunnes Stores

Hint of peachy aroma and flavours cut through by citrus-type acidity. Fruity off-dry finish. Chardonnay in the blend adds good texture.

Moyston Sémillon/Chardonnay 94   13
                                        Dunnes Stores

Typical example of this style. Exotic fruit tones cut through by pleasant lemon-type acidity.

Whites from £4.50 to £5.25

Hardy's Stamp Collection Sémillon/Chardonnay 94 14
(Allied Drinks)   *Widely available*
Good citrus-type fruit flavours and medium long finish.

McWilliam's Inheritance Colombard/Chardonnay 94
                                                  13
                                        Quinnsworth

Deep yellow in colour. Something different. Clear crisp nose and lean fruit backed up with lively acidity.

Tollana Chardonnay 94   12
Quinnsworth
Hints of melon with a racy lime acidity. Just enough length to make it interesting.

Whites from £5.25 to £6.50

Barramundi Sémillon/Chardonnay nv   13
(Woodford Bourne)   *Widely available*
Easy-drinking wine with sherbet aromas and flavours.

Brown Brothers Chenin Blanc 93   14
(Woodford Bourne)   *Widely available*
Typical damp wool Chenin aroma. Grapefruit-type flavours with good length on the finish.

Coldridge Chenin Blanc/Chardonnay 94   12
(Cassidy)   *Widely available*
Lively and crisp with some fruit appeal.

Hardy's Nottage Hill Chardonnay 94   13
(Allied Drinks)   *Widely available*
Subtle oak tones mark this easy-drinking, uncomplicated wine.

Hardy's RR Medium Dry 93   14
(Allied Drinks)   *Widely available*
Hints of peach and refreshing acidity. Medium sweet.

Jacob's Creek Sémillon/Chardonnay 94   13
(Fitzgeralds)   *Widely available*
Hard to beat for the quality/price ratio. Only wine snobs look down their noses at this one.

McWilliams Hanwood Chardonnay 94   13
Quinnsworth
Deep yellow gold. Good fruit in a 'cool' Aussie style. Has perfect balance between fruit and acidity.

Old Triangle Riesling 94   12
(Findlaters)   *Wine merchants/off licences*
Off-dry style. Good fruit development cut through with
crisp acidity.

Old Triangle Sémillon/Chardonnay 94   13
(Findlaters)   *Wine merchants/off licences*
Pale gold in colour with rich fruit reminiscent of kiwi.
Promise holds right through to the flavoursome finish.

Rosemount Sémillon/Chardonnay 94   13
(Grants)   *Widely available*
Golden-tinged with exotic fruit and long length of
flavour.

Whites between £6.50 and £8

Arunda Sémillon/Chardonnay 93   12
(Mackenway)   *Widely available*
Balanced oak tones. Attractive easy-drinking style.

Brown Brothers Dry Muscat 93   13
(Woodford Bourne)   *Widely available*
Spicy and crisp—perfect for pre-dinner drinks.

Carlyle Estate Chardonnay 93   14
(Greenhills)   *Widely available*
Reminiscent of pineapples. Spicy new oak tones with a
lingering finish.

Houghton Dry White 94   13
                                                    Mitchells
Chenin Blanc, Chardonnay, Sémillon and American oak.
Well-rounded smooth wine with a dry finish. Fruit cuts
through acidity but it fights back.

Jacob's Creek Chardonnay 94   13
(Fitzgeralds)   *Widely available*
Full of fruit cocktail tones and limey acidity.

A GREAT AUSTRALIAN ACHIEVEMENT

JACOB'S CREEK®
AUSTRALIA'S AWARD WINNING WINES

Krondorf Sémillon 95 13
(James Adams) *Wine merchants/off licences*
Grassy overtones with good weight and texture on the
palate. Has a touch of class.

McWilliams Mt Pleasant Chardonnay 93 14
Quinnsworth
Deep yellow/gold in colour and very Australian in style
with its exotic fruit tones.

McWilliams Mt Pleasant Elizabeth Sémillon 90 13
Quinnsworth
For the ABC (anything but Chardonnay) drinker. Low
alcohol. Creamy tones even though there is no oak
influence.

Mitchelton Estate Chardonnay 94 12
(Cassidy) *Widely available*
Kiwi fruit tones and lengthy aftertaste.

Mitchelton Estate Marsanne 93 14
(Cassidy) *Wine merchants/off licences*
Peachy fruit with lemon peel and honey overtones.
Something different.

Oxford Landing Sauvignon Blanc 94 14
(Findlaters) *Wine merchants/off licences*
Delicious creamy gooseberry fruits with plenty of bite.

Rosemount Estate Chardonnay 94 13
(Grants) *Widely available*
Deep golden with an intense exotic fruit character. Lively
acidity makes for a long refreshing finish. Typical Aussie
Chardonnay.

Rosemount Estate Fumé Blanc 94 14
(Grants) *Widely available*
Creamy rhubarb or gooseberry? Decide for yourself.
Good on its own as an apéritif.

Tyrrells Chardonnay 94   12
(Remy)   *Widely available*
Typical Australian style with ripe melon and pineapple
flavours in a straightforward style with a hint of spritz.

Wolf Blass Sémillon/Sauvignon Blanc 94   13
(Dillons)   *Widely available*
Nice balance of fruit and acidity. Good length.

Yaldara Chardonnay 93   12
(Barry & Fitzwilliam)   *Widely available*
Deep yellow in colour. Lots of oak influence. Finishes on
a fruity note.

Whites between £8 and £10

Barwang McWilliams Chardonnay 94   14
                                      Quinnsworth
Delicious toasty finish marks this wine which delivers on
fruit and lively limey acidity.

Blue Pyrenees Estate Chardonnay 93   13
(Remy)   *Widely available*
Deeply coloured. Aromas of pineapple and cream carry
through on flavour.

Brands Laira Chardonnay 94   14
                                      Quinnsworth
Smoky bacon tones from barrel fermentation with
lemon-type acidity. Very pleasant drinking.

Brown Brothers Chardonnay 93   13
(Woodford Bourne)   *Widely available*
Four months' maturation in new oak gives a creamy
tone. Well made and balanced.

Chateau Tahbilk Chardonnay 92   14
(United Beverages)   *Widely available*
Well balanced with harmonious fruit and acidity.
Complex finish reminiscent of a Burgundy style.

d'Arenberg Barrel-fermented Chardonnay 94   14
(Taserra)   *Widely available*
Big, rich and full-bodied, needing time to harmonise the
strong oak influence. Fine and balanced with creamy
fruits ending in a flavoursome but not overpowering
finish.

Hardy's Padthaway Chardonnay 93   14
(Allied Drinks)   *Widely available*
Deep golden in colour. Peach-like aromas with subtle oak
influence.

Krondorf Chardonnay 94/5   13
(James Adams)   *Wine merchants/off licences*
Lively melon flavours cut through with lemon peel
acidity.

Penfolds Koonunga Hill Chardonnay 94   13
(Fitzgeralds)   *Wine merchants/off licences*
Another good example of Chardonnay with exotic fruit
character.

★**Preece Chardonnay 94**   15
(Cassidy)   *Widely available*
A top example of Chardonay from Australia. Generous in
flavour with excellent fruit and acid balance. Subtle,
classy finish with a smack of toast.

Rothbury Estate Chardonnay 93   14
(Woodford Bourne)   *Widely available*
Luscious ripe fruit overlain with nuances of vanilla oak.
Long silky finish.

Wolf Blass Barrel-fermented Chardonnay 94   14
(Woodford Bourne)   *Widely available*
Tropical fruits. A long flavoursome finish with toasty
overtones.

Yalumba Family Reserve Chardonnay 94 13
(Findlaters) *Wine merchants/off licences*
Toasty subtle oak tones with very pleasant melon and
pear-like flavours. Crisp finish.

Whites between £10 and £12

★**Cape Mentelle Sémillon/Sauvignon 94** 15
(Findlaters) *Wine merchants/off licences*
Instantly appealing. Concentrated hint of gooseberry
shines through the fruit tones ending in a long finish.
Top quality.

Orlando St Hilary Padthaway Chardonnay 93 13
(Fitzgeralds) *Widely available*
Saffron in colour with lots of pineapple-type fruits. An
up-front wine—in colour, flavour and finish.

★**Rosemount Estate Show Reserve Chardonnay 93** 15
(Grants) *Wine merchants/off licences*
Big, fat buttery fruit wraps around harmonious citrus-
type acidity to give a long finish.

Rothbury Estate Sauvignon Blanc 94 13
(Woodford Bourne) *Widely available*
Creamy gooseberry tones with a delicious bite of limey
acidity and good length of flavour.

Whites between £12 and £15

Eileen Hardy Padthaway Chardonnay 93 14
(Allied Drinks) *Widely available*
Barrel-fermented and matured. Subtle pineapple
flavours with a nice tang of citrus acidity and a pleasant
spicy finish.

Hollick Chardonnay 93 14
(Kevin Parsons) *Pomeroys*
Rich warm fruit with lots of toasty oak and an interest-
ing pleasant spicy finish.

White between £15 and £20

★**Rosemount Estate Roxburgh 92**   15
(Grants)   *Widely available*
Glorious in colour and taste. Delicious luscious fruit
tones and tangy citrus acidity.

RED WINES

Reds under £4.50

Moyston Cabernet/Shiraz 93   14
     Dunnes Stores

Deep garnet colour. Plenty of blackcurrant and spicy
fruit aromas and flavours ending in a long satisfying
finish.

Seppelt Gold Label nv   14
     Dunnes Stores

Roasted red berry fruits. Something different at a good
price.

Reds between £4.50 and £5.25

Jacob's Creek Shiraz/Cabernet 94   12
(Fitzgeralds)   *Widely available*
The brand that started it all. To get a good understanding
of fruit-driven wines, start here.

McWilliam's Inheritance Shiraz/Cabernet nv   12
     Quinnsworth

Aromas reminiscent of cold tea-leaves. Easy-drinking
style with fruity flavours cutting through acidity.

Tollana Cabernet/Shiraz 93   14
     Quinnsworth

Minty tones that carry through on the palate. Good
length of flavour on finish.

Reds between £5.25 and £6.50

Barramundi Shiraz/Merlot nv 12
(Woodford Bourne) *Widely available*
Easy drinking, fruity wine. Ripe berry fruits.

Brown Brothers Tarrango 94 13
(Woodford Bourne) *Widely available*
Pioneered by Brown Brothers, Tarrango is the name of
the grape. Beaujolais style. Fruity and easy to drink. Best
served cool.

Coldridge Shiraz/Cabernet 94 13
(Cassidy) *Widely available*
Jammy fruits with good flavour development that
lingers.

Hardy's Nottage Hill Cabernet Sauvignon/Shiraz 93 13
(Allied Drinks) *Widely available*
Juicy fruit with minty overtones and good use of oak
giving length of flavour.

Old Triangle Shiraz 93 13
(Findlaters) *Widely available*
Blackberry and spice characterise this very approachable
wine. Deep purple tones.

Rosedale Ridge Cabernet Sauvignon 91 13
(Barry & Fitzwilliam) *Widely available*
Good concentration of fruit with a medium intense
finish.

Rosemount Shiraz/Cabernet Sauvignon 94 13
(Grants) *Widely available*
A good partnership. Shiraz adds the colour and spice
while Cabernet imparts good tannins and grip.

★**Seppelt Gold Label Cabernet Sauvignon 93** 15
Dunnes Stores
Hearty ripe blackcurrant flavour with oak tones hidden

behind. Harmonious with structure and length to the opulent finish.

Reds between £6.50 and £8

Arunda Cabernet Sauvignon 92   11
(Mackenway)   *Wine merchants/off licences*
Fruity and easy-drinking—good party wine!

Carlyle Estate Cabernet Sauvignon 92   13
(Greenhills)   *Widely available*
Very typical eucalyptus/mint aroma, full-flavoured.
Look out for the sediment which stains the bottle.

McWilliams Cabernet Sauvignon 93   13
                                      Quinnsworth
Deep blackberry aroma which follows through on
flavour. Tannin adds structure.

McWilliams Hanwood Cabernet Sauvignon 93   14
                                      Quinnsworth
Minty overtones with lots of fruit attack ending in a long
flavoursome finish.

Mitchelton Estate Shiraz 93   13
(Cassidy)   *Wine merchants/off licences*
Deep inky black colour. Fruity flavours jump out of the
glass.

Oxford Landing Cabernet Sauvignon/Shiraz 93   13
(Findlaters)   *Wine merchants/off licences*
Ripe blackberry fruits and balanced acidity add a rich
tone to this wine.

Rosemount Estate Cabernet Sauvignon 93   14
(Grants)   *Widely available*
Like crushing loganberries in a glass. Totally fruit driven
with enough supple tannins and acidity to add interest.
Long, long finish.

Rosemount Estate Shiraz 94   13
(Grants)   *Widely available*
Deep saturation of almost blackberry colour. Big
opulent fruit flavours expand and fan out ending in a
touch of spice.

Tyrrells Cabernet/Merlot 93   13
(Remy)   *Widely available*
Pleasant minty tones with good attack of ripe fruits
followed by a long finish.

Wolf Blass Shiraz/Cabernet Sauvignon 92   14
(Dillons)   *Widely available*
Fruity, best served slightly cool. Blackcurrant Ribena
character.

Yaldara Shiraz Reserve 93   12
(Barry & Fitzwilliam)   *Widely available*
Good lively fruit on the nose. Sweet immediate attack,
short finish.

Reds between £8 and £10

Barwang McWilliams Shiraz 93   14
                                                     Quinnsworth
Dense and deep fruit. Extremely well-balanced and
elegant. Another top example of the new regional styles
emerging from Australia.

Blue Pyrenees Estate 90   12
(Remy)   *Widely available*
Produced from Cabernet Sauvignon, Merlot and Shiraz.
A minty tone dominates.

Brands Laira Shiraz 93   14
                                                     Quinnsworth
Top-quality Shiraz fruit with elegance and a long 'cool'
finish.

★**Brown Brothers Cabernet Sauvignon 92** 15
(Woodford Bourne) *Widely available*
Extremely attractive with its deep crimson colour, ripe
fruit flavours and lingering finish.

Brown Brothers Shiraz 93 14
(Woodford Bourne) *Widely available*
Good combination of black cherry with integrated
tannin and long finish.

❦**Chateau Tahbilk Cabernet Sauvignon 91** 15
(United Beverages) *Widely available*
Full-bodied, rich and opulent with red berry fruits and a
hint of chocolate.

d'Arenberg d'Arry's Original Shiraz/Grenache 91 12
(Taserra) *Widely available*
Good depth of colour. Vibrant fruity wine packed with
flavour in an easy-drinking style.

d'Arenberg High Trellis Cabernet Sauvignon 91 14
(Taserra) *Widely available*
Big in colour and fruity extract. A pleasant hint of minty
eucalyptus is obvious on the nose but more subtle than
most.

d'Arenberg Old Vine Shiraz 90 14
(Taserra) *Widely available*
A very good example of Australian Shiraz. Blackberry
fruits, rich peppery flavour and slight bitter-sweet
finish.

Hardy's Coonawarra Cabernet Sauvignon 92 14
(Allied Drinks) *Widely available*
Attractive chocolate and fruity flavours. Ripe tannins.

Penfolds Koonunga Hill Shiraz/Cabernet 93 13
(Fitzgeralds) *Wine merchants/off licences*
A good partnership. Continues to leave an impression
long after the last swallow.

Preece Cabernet Sauvignon 93   14
(Cassidy)   *Widely available*
Spicy toasty flavours which carry through to a long
finish.

★**Rothbury Shiraz 92**   15
(Woodford Bourne)   *Widely available*
Deep in colour and flavour with definite blackberry fruit
flavours on the finish. Ripe mature wine with strong
appeal.

**Yalumba Family Reserve Cabernet Sauvignon/Merlot
91**   13
(Findlaters)   *Wine merchants/off licences*
Good colour structure, instant fruit appeal and good
length.

Yalumba Family Reserve Shiraz 92   14
(Findlaters)   *Wine merchants/off licences*
Chunky ripe blackberry fruit with a streak of firm
tannin; vanilla aromas.

Reds between £10 and £12

★**d'Arenberg Ironstone Pressings 92**   15
(Taserra)   *Widely available*
Well-structured, deep and interesting with peppery
spice, intense red berry fruits all combining to give an
extra long supple finish. Shows how good Grenache and
Shiraz can be as a blend.

★**Orlando St Hugo Cabernet Sauvignon 91**   15
(Fitzgeralds)   *Widely available*
Delicious drinking. Blackberry shaken up with a hint of
liquorice. Top quality.

Penfolds Bin 128 Coonawarra Shiraz 91/2   13
(Fitzgeralds)   *Wine merchants/off licences*
Classic Shiraz style. Fruit tones that are very obvious but
don't overpower.

★**Rosemount Estate Show Reserve Cabernet Sauvignon 92**   15
(Grants)   *Widely available*
Everything from colour to fruit to tannin harmonises in a classy long finish. Superb.

Wolf Blass Cabernet Sauvignon 92   14
(Dillons)   *Widely available*
Hints of nutmeg and other spices. Smooth silky texture. Lingering finish.

Wolf Blass President's Selection Cabernet Sauvignon 91   14
(Dillons)   *Widely available*
Opulent style with generous fruit, a long finish and the complexity that ageing in bottle gives.

★**Wolf Blass President's Selection Shiraz 91**   15
(Dillons)   *Widely available*
Instantly appealing. Concentrated blackberry aromas mingle with spice and cedar. Superb mature mellow style.

Reds between £12 and £15

★**Cape Mentelle Cabernet Sauvignon 91**   15
(Findlaters)   *Wine merchants/off licences*
Limited availability but worth seeking out for its immense fruit with concentrated layers of differing aromas ending in a complex finish.

★**Eileen Hardy Padthaway Shiraz 91**   15
(Allied Drinks)   *Widely available*
Quality winemaking with use of American and French oak. Deep crimson colour and delightful minty (eucalyptus) aromas. Wonderful drinking.

Red between £20 and £30

★**Ravenswood Hollick Cabernet Sauvignon 91**   15
(Kevin Parsons)   *Pomeroys*
Excellent quality with rich blackcurrant fruit and
powerful length of flavour.

Austria

Following the wine scandals in 1985 the Austrian wine industry has now been completely revamped and, coupled with a new and vibrant generation of winemakers, Austria boasts one of the most comprehensive, stringent and well-policed wine laws in the world. Despite sharing similarity of grapes, styles and labelling with Germany, its warmer climate gives Austrian wines a more varied and full-bodied style than its German counterparts. Although slow to make a comeback, Austrian wines are gradually regaining lost ground and making quite an impact on the wine market.

Labels

All Austrian wines have a red and white striped 'Banderole' around the neck or over the cork ensuring that official quotas are not breached. The wines are graded according to ripeness and sugar content in ascending order of quality as follows: Tafelwein; Landwein; Qualitätswein; Qualitätswein Kabinett; Prädikatswein Spätlese; Auslese; Strohwein (grapes partly dried on straw mats); Eiswein; Beerenauslese; Ausbruch; Trockenbeerenauslese.

Trocken: Dry. *Halbtrocken:* Medium dry. *Halbsüss* or *Lieblich:* Medium sweet. *Süss:* Sweet.

Aideen Nolan

WHITE WINE

| White under £5.25 |

Servus Burgenland 93   11
(Barry & Fitzwilliam)   *Widely available*
Pleasant drinking with a touch of pithy grapefruit.
Unusual capsule.

Bulgaria

Bulgaria has been the most successful of the Eastern European countries in terms of exports, with 90 per cent of its crop sold outside the country. However, Bulgaria's ability to produce quality Cabernet Sauvignon and Merlot, and to a lesser extent Chardonnay, Riesling and Gewürztraminer at rock bottom prices hindered its move from the low-price point of entry wines for which it has become famous.

Bulgaria's indigenous red grapes are Gamza, Kadarka, Mavrud and Melnik. Its indigenous white grapes are Rkatsiteli and Dimiat.

It will be a pity if Bulgaria's commercial success proves a hazard to its more expensive and interesting wines.

Labels

In ascending order of quality: Country wines; Varietal wines with stated geographic origin (43 regions); Controliran wines (27 zones); Reserve wines and estate selections are indications of high quality.

WHITE WINES   *Aideen Nolan*

White under £4.50

Lyaskovets Muscat/Chardonnay nv   11
(Barry & Fitzwilliam)   *Widely available*
Hints of marmalade with good balance between the acidity and fruit.

Whites between £4.50 and £5.25

BVC Mehana nv   12
(Fitzgeralds)   *Widely available*
Distinct Muscat nose with fresh acidity and clean finish. Drink young and fresh!

BVC Sliven Chardonnay & Misket 94   13
(Fitzgeralds)   *Widely available*
The Misket grape (a cross between Dimiat and Riesling)
is unique to Bulgaria. Good floral tones and the lively
acidity of Riesling really break through.

RED WINES

Reds between £4.50 and £5.25

BVC Haskovo Merlot 90   14
(Fitzgeralds)   *Widely available*
Whiff of tobacco backed up on the palate with a smooth
velvet texture. Rich long finish.

BVC Sliven Cabernet Sauvignon 89   14
(Fitzgeralds)   *Widely available*
Rich and mature with good balance. Extremely popular.

Melnik Harsovo 89   12
(Barry & Fitzwilliam)   *Widely available*
Tile brick in colour, showing maturity. Stewed fruit
flavours with a firm finish.

Reds between £5.25 and £6.50

BVC Rousse Cabernet Sauvignon Reserve 89   14
(Fitzgeralds)   *Widely available*
Opulent style with plummy chocolate aromas and
flavours. American oak ageing adds a hint of coconut.

Oriachovitza Cabernet Sauvignon Reserve 90   14
Mitchells
Lots of plummy fruit tones with a good bite of acidity
holding up the drying tannins. Well balanced with good
structure.

California
and Oregon

In the second half of the nineteenth century California was making quite a reputation for its wines until the appearance of the dreaded louse phylloxera, which ravaged the vineyards. These vineyards were capable of fine wine production from grapes known as *vitis vinifera*. To add to the area's woes, strong anti-alcohol sentiment culminated in the 'dry era' of Prohibition, which began in 1920. Then there was the Depression of 1929. The comfort of alcohol might have been of some minor relief to the population in the midst of the worst financial blight ever to hit the USA, but that was not to be. However, the vinification of wines for medicinal and ecclesiastical purposes was permitted.

With the repeal of Prohibition, the Second World War intervened and minds were focused on things other than winemaking. By the time prosperity returned, another generation had grown up with little knowledge of a culture involving fine wine and food. Out of all this there is one lesson the Californians learned. They could start from scratch, as there was no Old World tradition to hold back creativity; nor were they hidebound by existing rules. Indeed there is a parallel here with Australian winemakers. So the great adventure started.

California doesn't have a cool climate, and is generally scorched by the sun, but there are certain relieving factors. Just offshore is the ice-cold Humboldt current which acts for all the world like a refrigerator cooling the coast of southern California. An added bonus is created by the gaps in the coastal ranges forced through by the rivers heading for the ocean, the largest of which is the mile-wide mouth of San Francisco Bay. All these elements of terrain, chill winds, fog and sun bring about micro-climates where vineyards can flourish and produce fine wines.

The most famous wine areas are to be found dotted around San Francisco Bay, where names like Napa Valley,

Sonoma, Mendocino, to name but a few, are well known and respected world-wide.

As well as these vine-growing areas, there is Carneros down by the Bay and the numerous mountainside vineyards above the Napa floor, the Sierra Foothills, Central Valley, North Central Coast and South Central Coast.

And so it was in the 1960s that wineries like Mondavi and Heitz, to mention just two of a small number of creators, began to show the Old World that these vineyards had arrived. What better way to do so than by a head-to-head competition with the best of Bordeaux and Burgundy in 1976 in a blind tasting and run away with the top prizes? A new era was born, new wineries were opened and wine production from table wine through commercial quality to fine wines became a reality. Because of the capacity to match price with quality, success was assured.

It is heartening to see that the grape varieties used are not exclusively those of Bordeaux and Burgundy, but include Rhône varieties like Syrah, Viognier, Marsanne and Roussanne. Indeed, varieties from Spain, Italy and Portugal may be the new stars, not necessarily in the highest firmament but producing wines of excellent quality ready for immediate to medium-term drinking at very affordable prices. Production now is such that the home market is fully catered for and producers are turning to export markets. Robert Mondavi said some time ago that it would take twenty years to really convince the world that Californian wines are equal to the best anywhere, just as it took more than twenty-five years to convince the domestic market. So, notwithstanding the present weakness of the dollar, the consensus is that producers with a long-term pricing strategy and a philosophy of expansion will continue their efforts.

Although the application of inventiveness and new wine technology has been the backbone of success in California, the winemakers are still conscious of, if not necessarily dependent on, the Old World, particularly France, for their final guiding parameters in style.

Noel Kierans

WHITE WINES

Whites under £5.25

Ernest & Julio Gallo Chardonnay nv 12
(Fitzgeralds) *Widely available*
Good straightforward drinking with kiwi fruit and some
length to the finish.

Glen Ellen Proprietor's Reserve Sauvignon Blanc 94 14
(Grants) *Widely available*
Hearty fruit. Heads towards gooseberry and cream with
good balancing acidity.

Paul Masson Vintners Selection nv 11
(Dillons) *Widely available*
Uncomplicated easy-drinking fruity wine.

Whites between £5.25 and £6.50

Ernest & Julio Gallo Fumé Blanc nv 14
(Fitzgeralds) *Widely available*
Creaminess with hints of rhubarb make this an enjoyable
easy-drinking wine.

Ernest & Julio Gallo Sauvignon Blanc nv 13
(Fitzgeralds) *Widely available*
Good ripe Sauvignon fruit with lemon-type acidity
leaving a fresh finish.

Glen Ellen Proprietor's Reserve Chardonnay 93 14
(Grants) *Widely available*
Creamy in colour and creamy in taste, peachy vanilla
tones and a long finish.

Whites between £6.50 and £8

★ **Beringer Fumé Blanc 93** 16
(Allied Drinks) *Widely available*
Seductive wine with pronounced toasty oak aroma and
flavour. Note the hint of spice on the flavoursome finish.

Fetzer Fumé Blanc 93   13
(Ecock)   *Widely available*
Definite aniseed tones with crisp lively fruit and a
smooth finish.

Whites between £8 and £10

Allen Family Chardonnay nv   13
                                                   Mitchells
Creamy melons with medium acidity and buttery tones.

Buena Vista Carneros Chardonnay 91   14
(Greenhills)   *Widely available*
Pineapple and citrus flavours with a nice round and
balanced finish.

Clos du Val Le Clos Chardonnay 92   14
                                                   Terroirs
Classic style with a smooth attack of peachy fruit backed
up with balanced citrus-type acid. Hard to believe there
is no hint of oak.

Fetzer Sundial Chardonnay 92   13
(Ecock)   *Widely available*
Creamy soft melon-type fruits which linger long after
the last swallow.

Lillie Langtry Guenoc Chardonnay 93   13
(Remy)   *Widely available*
Delightful melon-type fruits that attack, persist and
linger on the finish. Balanced and well made.

Robert Mondavi Sauvignon Blanc 92   13
(Woodford Bourne)   *Widely available*
Elegant drink which tastes better on the palate than is
promised by the aroma. Medium acidity gives a
rounded finish.

David Dennison Fine Wines
The Wine Vault

WINE BAR & BISTRO, WINE SHOP

High Street, Waterford, Ireland.
el (051) 53444/53777 Fax (051) 53444 FaxMdem(051)53777

Graham's National Wine List of the Year Awards
Munster Regional Winner 1994/1995
Egon Ronay Recommended

The Best
New World & French Wine Selection
in Ireland

Agents for:
Mountadam and David Wynn Wines (Australia)
for Ireland, North & South

White between £10 and £12

Robert Mondavi Fumé Blanc 92   13
(Woodford Bourne)   *Wine merchants/off licences*
Melon and creamy fruit flavours with good crisp
acidity.

White between £12 and £15

Fetzer Barrel Select Chardonnay 90   14
(Ecock)   *Widely available*
A big mouthful of delicious, exotic fruit with nice limey
acidity giving a clean refreshing finish.

White between £15 and £20

★**Robert Mondavi Chardonnay 93**   15
(Woodford Bourne)   *Widely available*
Top quality with delicious oak and ripe tropical fruit
flavours wrapped around a nutty slightly spicy finish
balanced by good acidity.

RED WINES

Reds under £5.25

**Glen Ellen Proprietor's Reserve Cabernet Sauvignon
92**   12
(Grants)   *Widely available*
Smoky blackcurrant flavours accompany light tannins
and balanced acidity.

Paul Masson Vintners Selection nv   11
(Dillons)   *Widely available*
Soft, supple, easy-drinking.

Red between £5.25 and £6.50

Ernest & Julio Gallo Cabernet Sauvignon nv   13
(Fitzgeralds)   *Widely available*
Light in style. Juicy fruity appeal with good length of
flavour on the finish.

Reds between £6.50 and £8

★★**Beringer Zinfandel 91**   16
(Allied Drinks)   *Widely available*
Big opulent plummy fruit with great balance and superb colour.

Blossom Hill Cabernet Sauvignon nv   13
(Gilbeys)   *Widely available*
Easy-drinking with hints of oak in an uncomplicated style.

★**Fetzer Valley Oaks Cabernet Sauvignon 91**   15
(Ecock)   *Widely available*
Generous chunky Cabernet Sauvignon. Plummy and opulent with a long finish.

Fetzer Zinfandel 93   14
(Ecock)   *Widely available*
Still young but displaying meaty tones reminiscent of cooked roast beef.

Wente Bros Cabernet Sauvignon 94   14
(Cassidy)   *Widely available*
Good straightforward herbal and cassis tones. Nice development of oak on palate, smooth with a pleasant flavoursome finish.

Reds between £8 and £10

Allen Family Red Table Wine nv   13
Mitchells
Warm spicy fruit aromas with rich fruit attack span out on the palate and end in a long elegant finish.

Lillie Langtry Guenoc Cabernet Sauvignon 89   14
(Remy)   *Widely available*
A treat to drink with its eucalyptus tones, excellent ripe fruits and long length.

Robert Mondavi Woodbridge Cabernet Sauvignon 92
(Woodford Bourne)   *Widely available*   13
Recalls the scent of carrageen moss. It has elegance but
is quite short on the finish.

Reds between £12 and £15

★**Fleur de Carneros Pinot Noir 93**   15
(Kevin Parsons)   *Wine merchants/off licences*
Superb. Rich Pinot fruit flavours reminiscent of straw-
berry. Long finish.

★**Los Carneros Creek Pinot Noir 92**   15
(Kevin Parsons)   *Wine merchants/off licences*
Ripe and delicious flavours of raspberry and plums. A
tangy bite of refreshing acidity. Underlying tannin adds
structure.

★**Niebaum-Coppola Cabernet Sauvignon 92**   15
Terroirs
The winery is owned by the film director Francis Ford
Coppola. This Cabernet has just a hint of cherry and
mint in aroma but the fruit explodes on the palate. Well
structured—opulent. A big, almost chewy, wine.

Robert Mondavi Pinot Noir 91   13
(Woodford Bourne)   *Widely available*
Tile brick in colour with concentrated mature savoury
tones characteristic of Pinot. Glides over the palate and
finishes with lingering fruit.

Reds between £15 and £20

Robert Mondavi Cabernet Sauvignon 88   14
(Woodford Bourne)   *Widely available*
Bouquet due to bottle age with complex aromas of rich
cassis fruit on the palate and a long harmonious finish.

Reds between £30 and £50

★★Dominus Estate 85 16

Searsons

Superb quality. The elegance and finesse of classic
French winemaking partnered with Californian fruit
from Christian Moueix of Pomerol and the Inglenook
winery. Intense and impressive.

Red over £50

★★Opus One 91 16

(Woodford Bourne) *Widely available*

A joint venture between Robert Mondavi and Baronne
Philippine de Rothschild, this wine is bursting with
style. Dense and deep with smoky mineral tones. Plenty
of cassis fruit with elegant tannins and a long assertive
finish. Value for money? Probably not. But value for
taste experience? Definitely.

ROSÉ WINES

Rosé under £6.50

Blossom Hill White Zinfandel nv 12

(Gilbeys) *Widely available*

Easy drinkability in an off-dry finish. Serve chilled to
highlight the fruits.

Oregon

Oregon, located in Washington State, produces some of the
best fruity Pinot Noir outside Burgundy.

RED WINE

Red between £20 and £30

★Domaine Drouhin 91 15

(Gilbeys) *Wine merchants/off licences*

Has more fruit appeal than its Burgundian counterparts.
A silky texture and delicious long finish set it apart.

Chile

Chile is considered the showcase of South American wine production. The snow-covered Andes mountains guarantee vital water supplies for irrigation.

The Spanish conquistadores introduced wine production to the area in the mid-sixteenth century, and Jesuit missionaries helped it to spread, as they needed wine for sacramental purposes. Before their defeat by the Spanish, the Incas built an astonishing network of canals, which is one of the best water distribution systems in the world. This was vital for the development of viticulture areas in otherwise barren conditions, as it provides access to water from melted snows during the growing season.

Chile is almost unique in the wine world, as all its vines are free from the ravages of the phylloxera louse which devastated most of the world's vineyards in the latter half of the nineteenth century. The vineyards of Chile are protected from this plague by natural boundaries: to the west the cold Humboldt current in the Pacific, to the north the Atacama desert, to the east the Andes. This louse still poses a threat to vineyards elsewhere in the world. Vines in Chile are grown on their natural roots and can be productive for a hundred years rather than the average thirty to thirty-five.

Chile has good deep limestone soil and little rain, which falls mainly in winter. It makes world-class Cabernet Sauvignon, and (since 1989) Chardonnay. Wines are often made using Bordeaux techniques. Cabernet Sauvignon or Cabernet Sauvignon blends dominate red wine production. They can be fruity and lightweight or full-bodied and powerful and are often extremely good value for early drinking. White wines should be drunk very young, as they do not have the ability to age.

There are three significant winemaking areas in Chile. The first is Casablanca, near Valparaiso on the coast, where

THIS WEEKEND EXPLORE THE ANDES

Take as your guide, Aurelio Montes, one of South America's greatest wine-makers. In the shadow of the Andes, he has fashioned Ireland's most popular Chilean wines, Villa Montes Sauvignon Blanc and Cabernet Sauvignon.

MONTES
FROM CHILE
FINE NEW WORLD WINES

the climate is cooler due to morning fog and cloud. Fresh fruity white wines are made here, the main producers being Errázuriz and Concha y Toro.

The central valley, located north and south of Santiago, is the main production area. Good red wines are produced mostly from classic varieties, Cabernet Sauvignon, Cabernet Franc, Malbec and Merlot. Some Sauvignon Blanc and Chardonnay are also made. The main producers are Santa Rita, Santa Carolina, Undurraga, Cousiño Macul, Montes, Concha y Toro, Los Vascos, Canepa, Carmen, Santa Monica and Santa Helena.

The southern region, near Curicó and Talca, produces white wines of more finesse, due to the cooler climate. The main producer here is San Pedro.

Breda McSweeney

WHITE WINES

White under £4.50

Valdezaro nv 13
(Barry & Fitzwilliam) *Widely available*
Light in an easy-drinking style. Hints of marzipan on the nose.

Whites between £4.50 and £5.25

Caliterra Chardonnay 95 13
Quinnsworth
Good attack of fruit which fans out on the palate. Value for money.

Caliterra Sauvignon Blanc 94/5 12
Quinnsworth
Yellow gold in colour. Exotic aromas and flavours leaning towards ripe melon. Drink as young as possible.

Carta Vieja Sauvignon Blanc 94 12
(Barry & Fitzwilliam) *Widely available*
Tart apple fruit with a refreshing finish. Pleasant easy drinking.

Carta Vieja Sauvignon/Chardonnay 93   12
(Barry & Fitzwilliam)   *Widely available*
Unusual combination which refreshes but finishes short.

Undurraga Sauvignon Blanc 94   12
(United Beverages)   *Widely available*
Uncomplicated fresh style of herbaceous Sauvignon.
Good acidity and medium finish.

Villa Montes Sauvignon Blanc 94   12
(Grants)   *Widely available*
Clean and fresh-tasting even if it doesn't sing herbaceous
Sauvignon.

Whites between £5.25 and £6.50

Alondra Sauvignon 94   12
     Mitchells
Ripe in tone with a good attack of fruit intensity and
some lingering flavours.

Carmen Chardonnay 94   13
(Dillons)   *Widely available*
Appealing light gold in colour with hints of melon on the
nose which carry through on flavour.

Carmen Sauvignon Blanc 94   13
(Dillons)   *Widely available*
Fresh tasty Sauvignon in a vegetal style.

Cousiño-Macul Sauvignon Blanc 94   14
(Ecock)   *Widely available*
Classic structure with grassy tones and a nice spicy bite
to the finish.

Errázuriz Chardonnay 93   14
(Allied Drinks)   *Widely available*
Lots of subtle oak gives this wine great appeal. It
delivers on both flavour and length.

Errázuriz Sauvignon Blanc 94   13
(Allied Drinks)   *Widely available*
Typical Chilean Sauvignon with its zesty acidity,
gooseberry fruit and long finish.

Errázuriz Sauvignon Blanc Reserva 92   14
(Allied Drinks)   *Widely available*
Hint of turmeric spice. Subtle oak influence and good
length.

Miguel Torres Santa Digna Sauvignon Blanc 94   14
(Woodford Bourne)   *Widely available*
Crisp and fresh with good herbaceous tones.

San Pedro Sauvignon Blanc 94   12
Dunnes Stores
Fresh with lively acidity and good fruit.

Santa Carolina Sauvignon Blanc 93   12
(Fitzgeralds)   *Wine merchants/off licences*
Pale in colour with ripe fruits reminiscent of pineapple.
Cut through by crisp acidity with a high alcohol finish.

Santa Helena Sauvignon Blanc 94   12
(Taserra)   *Widely available*
Good price/quality ratio. Zesty herbaceous style
associated with Sauvignon Blanc.

Santa Ines Chardonnay 94   14
(Mackenway)   *Widely available*
Pineapple springs to mind. A long satisfying finish.

Santa Rita 120 Sauvignon Blanc 94   12
(Gilbeys)   *Widely available*
Good weight for a Sauvignon and less herbaceous than
most. Good attack of fruit ending in a medium short
finish.

★**Vina Porta Chardonnay 94**   15
(Searsons)   *Wine merchants/off licences*
Delicious! Six months' maturation on the lees (sediment)
imparts a creamy yeastiness with rich fruit and good
length.

Whites between £6.50 and £8

Caliterra Chardonnay Reserva 93   14
Quinnsworth
Lots of subtle fruity aroma and flavours backed up with
a pleasant toasty finish.

Concha y Toro Casillero del Diablo Chardonnay 93   13
(Findlaters)   *Widely available*
Nutty and creamy with good use of oak. A satisfying
drink.

Cono Sur Chenin Blanc 93   12
(Greenhills)   *Widely available*
Just enough fruit and acid balance for easy drinking.

Cono Sur Sauvignon Blanc 93   12
(Greenhills)   *Widely available*
A middleweight wine with a hint of fruit flavours.

Cousiño-Macul Chardonnay 94   14
(Ecock)   *Widely available*
Reminiscent of corned beef on the nose, with a mouth-
filling flavoursome finish.

Santa Carolina Special Reserve Sauvignon Blanc 93   13
(Fitzgeralds)   *Wine merchants/off licences*
Fermented in new French oak. Maintains its gooseberry
fruit tones and is cut through by crisp acidity.

**Santa Helena Seleccion del Directorio Oak-aged
Chardonnay 93**   14
(Taserra)   *Widely available*
Green gold in colour, the oak and fruit sing a duet, with

a pleasant citrus acidity. A touch of spice from the new
oak ends on a high note.

Santa Helena Siglo de Oro Chardonnay 94   13
(Taserra)   *Widely available*
Young, fresh and lively. Packed with ruby grapefruit
flavours that linger.

★**Santa Ines Chardonnay Reserva 94**   15
(Mackenway)   *Widely available*
Fermenting in oak adds extra distinction to this well-
made wine which has good exotic fruit tones and lots of
vanilla creaminess.

> Whites between £8 and £10

★**Errázuriz Barrel Fermented Reserva Chardonnay 93** 15
(Allied Drinks)   *Widely available*
Harmonious use of oak allows the fruit to follow
through. Note the extra long creamy finish. Excellent.

Santa Carolina Special Reserve Chardonnay 93   14
(Fitzgeralds)   *Wine merchants/off licences*
Subtle use of oak in this wine imparts balance and
elegance. Leaving it in contact with its lees (sediment)
also adds complexity to the structure.

Santa Rita Medalla Real Chardonnay 93   13
(Gilbeys)   *Widely available*
Lots of colour and a good balance between fruit, acidity
and oak. Lingering fruit finish.

Santa Rita Medalla Real Sauvignon Blanc 93   14
(Gilbeys)   *Widely available*
Extra character and weight of fruit. Long fruity finish.

"Molloy's Liquor Stores brings the
world of wine to you.
Be adventurous - savour spicy
Rhones, opt for oaky Riojas, enjoy
the fruity flavours of Australian
varietals or the freshness of a
Chilean Sauvignon Blanc.
Experience our global tour!"

Catherine Griffith
Wine Consultant

RED WINES

Reds under £5.25

★**Caliterra Cabernet Sauvignon 93**   15
Quinnsworth

Deeply coloured with lots of blackberry jam fruit that
fans out on the palate. Great drinking at a very fair
price.

Carta Vieja Cabernet/Merlot 92   14
(Barry & Fitzwilliam)   *Widely available*
Merlot gives the colour and Cabernet the zap to this
wine dominated by good fruity flavour.

Carta Vieja Cabernet Sauvignon 92   13
(Barry & Fitzwilliam)   *Widely available*
Youthful purple colour tones with deep pepper-type
aromas. Pleasant drinking at a fair price.

Valdezaro nv   12
(Barry & Fitzwilliam)   *Widely available*
Typical capsicum or pea-pod nose. Good food wine.

Villa Montes Cabernet Sauvignon 92/3   14
(Grants)   *Widely available*
A deep saturation of crimson with lots of red berry fruit
aromas and a good smack of tannin.

Reds between £5.25 and £6.50

Alondra Cabernet Sauvignon 93   13
Mitchells

A good food wine. Spicy fruit that holds up on flavour.
Pleasant drinking.

★★**Carmen Cabernet Sauvignon 91**   16
(Dillons)   *Widely available*
Rich and wonderful with dense smoky aromas and lots
of fruit development. Powerful concentrated finish.

Carmen Merlot 92 14
(Dillons) *Widely available*
Produced from 100% Merlot. Deep ruby in colour with
intense fruit flavours and herbal nuances.

Cousiño-Macul Cabernet Sauvignon 93 14
(Ecock) *Widely available*
Herbal toned. Deep ruby colour with harmonious
balance between fruit and tannin. Satisfying finish.

Errázuriz Cabernet Sauvignon 93 14
(Allied Drinks) *Widely available*
Green pepper aromas with good flavours that continue
right through to the end.

★**Errázuriz Merlot 94** 16
(Allied Drinks) *Widely available*
Wins on all counts with its creamy plum flavours and a
rich concentrated finish. A savoury wine.

Miguel Torres Santa Digna Cabernet Sauvignon 91 14
(Woodford Bourne) *Widely available*
Ripe blackberry fruit flavours in an easy-drinking style.

San Pedro Cabernet Sauvignon 93 14
(Cassidy) *Widely available*
A smooth, green pepper-type Cabernet with good
development and strong finish.

Santa Carolina Cabernet Sauvignon/Merlot 92 13
(Fitzgeralds) *Wine merchants/off licences*
Well made with great depth of colour followed by
characteristic aromas of green pepper. Well structured.
Long finish, already throwing some sediment.

Santa Helena Cabernet Sauvignon 93 13
(Taserra) *Widely available*
Ruby in colour. Good texture and weight with capsicum
or green pepper aromas.

Santa Rita 120 Cabernet Sauvignon 94   14
(Gilbeys)   *Widely available*
Medium-bodied soft easy-drinking Cabernet—good
with or without food.

Santa Rita 120 Merlot 92   13
(Gilbeys)   *Widely available*
Easy-drinking Merlot. Smoky with jammy fruits and a
long finish.

Undurraga Cabernet Sauvignon Reserve 93   12
(United Beverages)   *Widely available*
Stalky Cabernet fruit with good colour and supple
tannins. Don't look for complexity—just enjoy.

Reds between £6.50 and £8

Caliterra Cabernet Sauvignon Reserva 92   14
Quinnsworth
Deep saturation of colour. Caraway seeds on aroma
with very good harmonious tannins. Fruit bursts out on
the finish.

**Concha y Toro Casillero del Diablo Special
Reserve 93**   14
(Findlaters)   *Wine merchants/off licences*
Generous amounts of ripe red berry fruit overlain with
spice. Well rounded and balanced.

★ **Cousiño-Macul Cabernet Sauvignon Antiguas
Reservas 91**   15
(Ecock)   *Widely available*
Classic structure. Intensely flavoured with a herb-like
bay leaf tone. Wonderful concentrated finish.

Montes Merlot 93/4   13
(Grants)   *Widely available*
Good bite of soft fruits with balanced acidity and just
enough tannin to add interest.

Santa Carolina Special Reserve Cabernet Sauvignon 90
                                                            14
 (Fitzgeralds)   *Wine merchants/off licences*
Liquorice tones with hints of cedar. Both American and
French oak influence. Needs more time to fulfil its
promise.

★ **Santa Carolina Special Reserve Merlot 92**   15
(Fitzgeralds)   *Wine merchants/off licences*
Classic Merlot. Plummy tobacco aromas with rich
supple tannins ending in a long smooth finish.

**Santa Helena Seleccion del Directorio Cabernet
Sauvignon 91**   14
(Taserra)   *Widely available*
Blackcurrant fruit with oak influence. Great depth of
flavour combined with a long rich finish.

Santa Helena Siglo de Oro Cabernet Sauvignon 93   12
(Taserra)   *Widely available*
Lean fruit in a medium-bodied style make this a pleasant
food wine.

Vina Porta Cabernet Sauvignon 91   14
(Searsons)   *Wine merchants/off licences*
French oak and Chilean know-how. Big in fruit flavours
with hints of tobacco and a touch of pleasant austerity
on the finish.

Reds between £8 and £10

Cousiño-Macul Maipo Merlot 91   14
(Ecock)   *Widely available*
Generous fruit flavours with a smoky overtone, rich and
satisfying.

★**Errázuriz Don Maximiano Estate Cabernet Sauvignon
Reserva 91**   15
(Allied Drinks)   *Wine merchants/off licences*
A rich wine with complex aromas of blackcurrant and

caraway seeds. Weighty in texture with a smooth lingering finish.

Santa Rita Medalla Real Cabernet Sauvignon 92   14
(Gilbeys)   *Widely available*
Smoky overtones from oak. A winner with its smooth silky texture and finish.

Red between £12 and £15

★**Montes Alpha 91**   15
(Grants)   *Widely available*
Another star in a classic style. Has the opulence of blackberry fruit with good weight on the palate and a long lingering finish with a smack of drying tannin.

Red between £15 and £20

★**Santa Rita Casa Real Cabernet Sauvignon 91**   15
(Gilbeys)   *Widely available*
Rich and concentrated with deep purple tones—wonderful cassis fruit and balanced oak appeal.

ROSÉ WINES

Rosé under £5.25

Valdezaro Blush nv   11
(Barry & Fitzwilliam)   *Widely available*
Pleasant off-dry, easy-drinking style.

Rosé between £5.25 and £6.50

Miguel Torres Santa Digna Cabernet Sauvignon Rosé 94   13
(Woodford Bourne)   *Widely available*
Pale cherry in colour. Plum and strawberry flavours ending in a dry finish give the wine instant appeal.

France

France produces the greatest amount of fine wine in the world, its reputation for quality wines having been built on the classic wines from Bordeaux and Burgundy, which have become role models for winemakers the world over. In reality these wines make up a very small percentage of overall production in France, but by their nature they have pulled lesser-known wines along on the marketing train, establishing a strong international following. However, the words 'Produce of France' stamped on a label are not in themselves a guarantee of quality.

Between the top end of the scale, where quality is unrivalled but beyond most people's budgets, and the bottom end, where the word 'plonk' was first heard, there is a huge middle section of wine which can surprise and delight. In 1994 estimated wine production in France was 55m hectolitres, of which 21.7m hectolitres was Appellation Contrôlée. This leaves a vast and often happy hunting ground in the mid-range quality level.

Over the centuries France has developed a highly sophisticated wine industry which is being constantly redefined. Geographically the country is well suited to growing the grape, falling as it does between latitudes 42 and 50 degrees—ideal for viticulture. Experimentation over hundreds of years has resulted in a greater understanding of different local climates and soils to suit different grape varieties. This accumulated knowledge, along with careful observation by wine growers of each grape's special characteristics, has enabled vines to be planted to suit particular *terroirs*. Terroir is the French philosophy that a wine reflects all the natural factors of where it is grown, e.g. soil type, micro-climate, exposure to sun, location and altitude of the vineyard. The French belief is that winemakers should aim to properly reflect all these elements in the final style of wine, imbuing it with its own

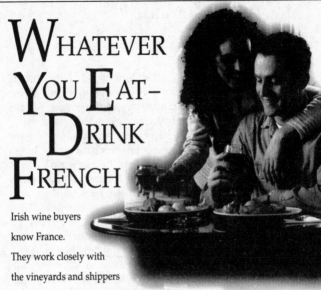

personality. For example the Syrah of the Rhône, Cabernet Sauvignon and Merlot of Bordeaux, Pinot Noir of Burgundy, Riesling of Alsace, Chardonnay of Champagne and Burgundy all produce wines with their geographical origin stamped on them.

Quality control has also played a major role in French winemaking. In the mid-nineteenth century wine production was seriously damaged by three major viticultural disasters in the form of two fungal diseases, oidium (powdery mildew) and peronospera (downy mildew), and the pest phylloxera, a louse that irreparably damages the vine by attacking the roots. European species of vines are highly susceptible to phylloxera, the only preventive measure being to graft European vines on to American root stocks. This all led to chaos, so regulations governing the actual vineyard region and covering the growing, making and storing of wine were redefined and enforced. Very detailed criteria were laid down to maximise quality and minimise fraud, which led to the establishment in 1930 of AOC (or AC) (Appellation d'Origine Contrôlée). Overseen by the INAO (Institut National des Appellations d'Origine), only grapes authorised and officially listed by the INAO can be used to produce Appellation Contrôlée wine. Rules are laid down regarding the spacing of vines, the yield at harvest time, and the planting, pruning and harvesting of grapes as well as the production and maturation of the wine.

Vins de Pays, which are regional country wines, are produced from grapes traditional to a particular region or from the so-called cépage ameliorators (classic varieties such as Syrah, Cabernet Sauvignon, Merlot, Chardonnay, Sauvignon Blanc. The wine grower can plant the vines he/she feels are best suited to particular local geographical conditions. Under this category, established in 1973 and formalised in 1979, wines can be sold as varietals (produced from 100 per cent of the grape variety stated) or as wines of a particular geographical origin, e.g. Vin de Pays du Jardin de la France (indicating the Loire region). It is fair to say that Vin de Pays allows greater flexibility.

Over the last couple of decades France has had more and more competition from top-quality wines from the New World (countries such as Australia, New Zealand, South America, North America and South Africa). This has led to a reappraisal of the industry, resulting in a mini-revolution in areas traditionally associated with basic Vin de Table. The quality category of Vin de Pays has, in less than two decades, brought a whole new dynamic to the industry. To give an example, between 1988 and 1993 more than 70,000 hectares of low-quality vines were uprooted under the Vine Pull Scheme.

Continued investment in modern winemaking technology and huge advances in modern communication have meant that France has woken up from its complacency and is beginning to kick back, producing new tastes in old places such as Languedoc-Roussillon, Provence and South-West France. Older vignerons who were slow to change traditional ways are passing on the business to more open-minded sons and daughters educated in the great wine universities of Bordeaux, Montpellier and Dijon, who have travelled to experience at first hand wine developments in other countries. So-called 'flying winemakers' from the New World descend at vintage time to make wine and offer advice. Modern communications such as the fax, the computer and high-speed travel have all ensured that new ideas are thought out and experimented with very quickly.

It is worth noting that AC still holds great importance in France for the winemaker and wine buyer. Unfortunately, what should be a guarantee of quality can often disappoint. The opposite is the case for Vin de Pays, where some stunning wines are being produced at great value.

However, even with all the modern technology at our disposal, such as state-of-the-art winemaking equipment, temperature control, etc. the fruit in the vineyard must achieve its optimum ripeness. It is this more than anything else that gives the final wine its personality. The classic areas will always have their rightful place in the hierarchy of wine, but demand is outstripping supply. This stimulates the production of better wines at better value in the mid-range categories.

Competition is strong and healthy, which must add up to greater benefits for the consumer in terms of choice and price. The future does indeed look exciting for the wine drinker providing that an uninteresting bland uniformity of wine styles doesn't become the norm! Whistle-clean wine lacking character is not the answer to long-term market needs. Let's hope that future trends will tend towards more interesting wine styles that combine modern technology with the French philosophy of terroir. This, then, is the way forward, the old with the new, which will ensure a greater diversity of wine styles for us all to enjoy. As they say, 'Vive la différence' and long live 'le bon petit vin' which in its way pays homage to 'le grand vin', which offers sublime if only occasional drinking pleasure.

Alsace

Bordering eastern France, Alsace is very picturesque, with vineyards laced around beautiful villages lying between the Vosges Mountains and the Black Forest. The region extends over two departments, Haut-Rhin and Bas-Rhin. Boasting one of the lowest annual rainfalls in France, the Vosges Mountains protect the vineyards from excessive rain. The wine trade is dominated by négociants (wine merchants) and co-operatives. There are thousands of small farmers with small landholdings growing grapes to sell on to the local co-ops, although some growers are now beginning to bottle their own wines.

Predominantly white, the wines of Alsace are named after the grape variety from which they are made and are not influenced by oak. More often seen on restaurant lists than wine shops, it is a pity that the consumer has not yet learnt to appreciate fully these great food wines, which are equally delicious served with European or Asian food. Other styles include rich unctuous sweet wines as well as red and sparkling wines. Easily identified in the long slim green bottle known as 'la flûte d'Alsace', these wines are packed with aromas of flowers and honey, full of refreshing acidity with a dry finish and long aftertaste.

By law all wines produced in Alsace are bottled in their region of origin. Edelzwicker or Vin d'Alsace on the label indicates that the wine has been blended from several varieties. Some producers indicate better wines by putting terms such as 'Cuvée spéciale' or 'Réserve personelle' on the label. Look out for the wines of Riesling, Gewürztraminer, Pinot Gris or Tokay d'Alsace, Muscat d'Alsace, Sylvaner and Pinot Blanc. Red and rosé wines are produced from the Pinot Noir grape.

If wine is produced from one of four grape varieties (Riesling, Gewürztraminer, Pinot Gris or Muscat), and if it comes 100 per cent from one of over 52 specifically named vineyards, it is entitled to carry the words *Grand Cru* on the label.

Sweet styles

Vendange Tardive (Late Harvested): To be entitled to use this term on the label wines must be made from late-picked berries which have attained an above average ripeness.

Selection de Grains Nobles: Wines produced from grapes that have a very high sugar content due to extended ripening and which in most cases have been affected by 'noble rot' (a beneficial fungus that concentrates the sugar levels) can be labelled with this term. The wines are rich and very complex with great ageing ability.

Sparkling

Crémant d'Alsace: Quality sparkling wine produced in the traditional way (champagne method). Mostly produced from the Pinot Blanc and Auxerrois grape varieties.

Wines from Alsace available in Ireland

Houses represented in Ireland include: F. E. Hugel, F. E. Trimbach, Zind Humbrecht, Caves de Turckheim, Dopff au Moulin, Domaines Schlumberger and Château d'Orschwihr.

WHITE WINES

White under £6.50

Wolfberger Pinot d'Alsace AC 94   12
Quinnsworth

Good balance of stony fruits with a fresh clean finish and just a hint of spice.

Whites between £6.50 and £8

Cave Hunawhir Pinot Blanc AC 93   13
(Searsons)   *Widely available*

Slight mineral tone on the nose. Flavoursome with an underlying edge of acidity.

Wolfberger Gewürztraminer AC 94   13
Quinnsworth

Rose petals all the way. Good fruit development with medium acidity and medium finish.

Whites between £8 and £10

Hugel Gewürztraminer AC 92   14
(Grants)   *Widely available*

Turkish Delight aromas with rich palate development. Shows great character with elegance and style. Medium acidity and long finish.

Hugel Riesling AC 91   14
(Grants)   *Widely available*

Good example of Riesling. Hint of maturity on the nose intrudes on the floral tone. Tingling acidity with extensive flavours. Long refreshing finish.

Trimbach Gewürztraminer AC 92   14
(Gilbeys)   *Widely available*

Turkish Delight aromas carry through on taste. A spicy finish with lavish acidity makes it a good choice with oriental cuisine.

Trimbach Riesling AC 92   13
(Gilbeys)   *Wine merchants/off licences*

Even though the acidity is a little high this is a good example of the careful balance between fruit and acidity of well-made Alsace Riesling.

Trimbach Tokay Pinot Gris Reserve AC 92   13
(Gilbeys)   *Widely available*

A good mouthful of fruit cut through by acidity makes a balanced wine with good length.

Turckheim Gewürztraminer AC 94   14
(Brangan)   *Wine merchants/off licences*
Rose petals and lychees abound with enough acidity,
spicy length and long flavoursome finish to merit
attention.

White between £10 and £12

Domaine Zind Humbrecht Sylvaner AC 93   14
(Brangan)   *Wine merchants/off licences*
One of the best Sylvaners available. Mineral overtone,
good fruit attack and enough crisp acidity to leave a
fresh finish.

Bordeaux

Located in South-West France, cut through by the Dordogne and Garonne rivers, Bordeaux can be broken into six main districts, within which are individual communes with their own appellations. The whole area stretches 90 miles north to south and 40 miles east to west, with a temperate climate. Covering over 100,000 hectares, all wines produced are Appellation d'Origine Contrôlée. Estimated wine production in 1994 was 5.4 million hectolitres.

Main classifications

The basic appellation of Bordeaux AC covers red and white wines from all over the region. Within the region, however, there are many districts entitled to their own individual appellations.

The Graves classification was created in 1953 and in 1987 a new appellation, Pessac-Léognan, was created to cover red and white wines of northern Graves. The St Emilion classification is for red wines only. Very well known and popular in Ireland, this appellation can be confusing. Established in 1955, it is revised every ten years or so. Two châteaux, Ausone and Cheval Blanc, are Class A Premier Grand Cru Classé wines. There are nine Class B Premier Grand Cru Classé wines and sixty-one Grand Cru Classé wines. St Emilion on the label indicates the general appellation for the area. Not offering quite the same complexity, some surrounding areas annex the name. These include Montagne St Emilion, St Georges St Emilion, Puisseguin St Emilion and Lussac St Emilion.

1855 classification

Most of Bordeaux's most famous communes are located within Haut-Médoc. St Estèphe, Pauillac, St Julien, Margaux, Listrac-Médoc and Moulis-en-Médoc are all entitled to their own appellation. Only red wines are produced here. The 1855 classification of the Médoc was intended as a guide for wines entered for the Great Paris Exhibition of 1855. Sixty-three châteaux were divided into five levels of excellence. Of these, only five—Ch Latour, Ch Lafite, Ch Margaux, Ch Haut-Brion (Pessac-Léognan) and Ch Mouton-Rothschild—are entitled to Premier Cru Classé status. Ch Mouton-Rothschild was elevated to this category only in 1973. The remaining wines or top châteaux were classified as second, third, fourth and fifth growths and are known collectively as Crus Classés. At this quality level vintage variation takes on special importance, as wines produced in good years can age for decades.

As the classed growths of Bordeaux are beyond most everyday drinking budgets, the claret lover should be aware of the large amount of quality red wines available at affordable prices. Take, for example, the Cru Bourgeois wines of the Médoc. Historically these were quality vineyards owned by the wealthy upper classes. Today Cru Bourgeois represents over 40% of all Médoc wines and includes over 160 properties.

Some terms explained

Château: The name given to a wine estate within the region growing the grape and producing the wine. Multinational corporations now own quite a few of the top châteaux.

Co-operatives: Producing over 30% of Bordeaux wines, co-operatives buy grapes and vinify the wine. They may also stock and mature wine before releasing it for sale.

Broker: The wine broker acts as a mediator between the growers and shippers.

Shipper: Buys wine to keep for a short period before placing it on the market under a commercial brand name or own brand.

Négociant-éleveur: A shipper who keeps wine and matures it for a long period before placing it on the market. Reliable négociants whose wines are available on the

Irish market are (listed in alphabetical order): Barton & Guestier (B & G), Calvet, Cordier, Cruse, Dourthe, Dulong, Eschenauer, Alexis Lichine, Gilbey de Loudenne, Borie Manoux, Schroder & Schyler, Sichel.

Vintage: The year in which the grapes were harvested and the wine made.

La Bordelaise: The traditional bottle for Bordeaux, now emulated all over the world.

Styles

Red and white wines vary in style from the great classified growths, the Crus Classés, which require time to mellow and mature, to earlier drinking styles. To understand Bordeaux wine it is important to remember that the wine is produced from several grape varieties.

For red wine Cabernet Sauvignon, Merlot, Malbec and Petit Verdot are used. Cabernet Sauvignon dominates production in the Médoc and Graves, Merlot in St Emilion and Pomerol. Sauvignon Blanc, Sémillon and Muscadelle are used for white wines. Wines produced from these grapes are blended in different proportions. With vintage variation a major factor from year to year, the 'mix' of grapes helps to create balance in the final wine. Other factors affecting the final style of wine are the age of the vines, the area of production and viticultural practices.

Generally speaking, Bordeaux wines fall into the following categories:

- Tannic reds needing time to mature
- Lighter reds made for early consumption
- Rich complex and lighter sweet wines
- Dry whites requiring time to mature
- Dry whites for early consumption
- Rosé
- Sparkling

Within these styles are some of the greatest wines in the

world and some of the most ordinary.

Years ago top-quality Bordeaux red wines were meant to mature for anything from ten to thirty years, but today wines are produced for earlier consumption. Big advances in the vineyard and the winery have ensured young Cru Classé wines becoming more approachable. There has also been an overall improvement in quality, even in the lesser-known appellations.

Bordeaux wines available in Ireland

Bordeaux: Red and white wines from the whole region.

Bordeaux Supérieur: Red, white and rosé wines. Supérieur indicates a wine with a slightly higher alcohol content.

Médoc: Red wines only.

Haut-Médoc: Red wines only. Cabernet Sauvignon dominates wine production.

Graves: Red and white wine production. The region gets its name from the gravelly soil of the area and its wines are reputed to have a certain earthy flavour. The most famous wine of Graves, Château Haut-Brion, is a Premier Cru Classé.

St Emilion: Red wine only. Merlot dominates wine production.

Pomerol: Red wines only, with Merlot dominant. Ch Pétrus, the most famous red wine of Pomerol, was never actually classified but is recognised internationally as one of the world's great red wines.

Fronsac: Red wines. Located west of St Emilion, it is considered by many experts to be waiting in the aisles and about to be re-discovered by the wine-drinking public who are looking for a classic style without breaking the bank. Vineyards located in the heart of the region are entitled to the Canon-Fronsac appellation and are considered higher in quality.

Entre-Deux-Mers: White wines only. Located between the Dordogne and the Garonne rivers, the wines should be drunk very young.

Cérons, Barsac, Sauternes, Cadillac, St Macaire, Ste Croix du

Mont: Appellations for sweet wines. Of these, Sauternes is the best known. Château d'Yquem, the world's most expensive sweet wine, is the only Premier Grand Cru Classé of the region.

Premières Côtes de Bordeaux: Medium sweet, white and red production.

Lesser-known but good-value appellations seen on the Irish market include: *Côtes de Francs* and *Côtes de Castillon* (red), *Lalande de Pomerol* (red), *Canon-Fronsac* (red), *Côtes de Bourg* and *Côtes de Blaye* (red and white).

WHITE WINES

Whites between £4.50 and £5.25

Calvet Sauvignon AC Bordeaux 94   13
(Grants)   *Widely available*
Good herbaceous attack. Slightly earthy tone. Some length. Should be drunk young.

Château Fleur Grand Champs AC Entre-Deux-Mers 94
                                        Quinnsworth   12
Good grassy tones with clean fresh acidity and green fruit flavours.

Domaine de Grand Pouget AC Bergerac 94   13
                                            Quinnsworth
Good blend of Sauvignon and Sémillon fruit with balanced lime acidity. Good length on the finish. Goes well with food.

Whites between £5.25 and £6.50

Château Timberlay AC Bordeaux 93   13
(James Adams)   *Wine merchants/off licences*
Good colour with a hint of ripe apple fruits backed up with length of flavour on the finish.

Fonset Lacour AC Bordeaux 93   12
(Dillons)   *Widely available*
Choose the latest vintage available to enjoy the freshness

of this wine which has ripe apple peel aroma and
freshness.

Louis de Camponac Sauvignon AC Bordeaux 94   13
Mitchells

Hint of elderflower aromas cut through with zesty
acidity, all ending in a fresh crisp finish.

Malesan Sec AC Bordeaux 93   12
(Taserra)   *Wine merchants/off licences*

Crisp and fresh wine with just a hint of apple fruits and
no oak influence.

Whites between £6.50 and £8

B & G Fondation 1725 AC Bordeaux 93   12
(Dillons)   *Widely available*

Fruity and fresh—at its best drunk young, so look for the
latest vintage.

Calvet Réserve AC Bordeaux 93   12
(Grants)   *Widely available*

'Fruity' describes this easy-drinking white with delicate
fruits and medium acidity.

Chai de Bordes-Quancard AC Bordeaux 94   13
(Brangan)   *Widely available*

Clean and fresh with hints of grapefruit and a crisp
finish.

Château Bonnet André Lurton AC Entre-Deux-Mers 94
(Febvre)   *Wine merchants/off licences*   14

Good example of this style. Full of herbaceous zesty
fruit and cut through with mouth-watering acidity.

Château de la Jaubertie AC Bergerac 94   13
Mitchells

A delicious bite of apple fruit in a dry fresh style.

Château la Freynelle AC Bordeaux 94   13
(Searsons)   *Widely available*

Good balance between fruit and acidity, texture and finish. Holds up on fruit and has some length on the finish.

★ **Château Tour de Mirambeau Jean Louis Despagne AC Bordeaux 93** 15
Wines Direct

This has it all! Upfront flavours of gooseberry with good balancing acidity and a delicious lingering finish.

Michel Lynch AC Bordeaux 93 12
(Barry & Fitzwilliam) *Widely available*
Hints of apricots. Straightforward in an easy-drinking style. Good with food.

Mouton Cadet AC Bordeaux 93 13
(Findlaters) *Widely available*
Reminiscent of ice cream wafers on the nose. Silky texture with good ripe apple fruit and balanced acidity.

White between £8 and £10

★**Château de Sours AC Bordeaux Supérieur 92** 15
Mitchells

Extremely appealing. Toasty oak and creamy peach tones are the hallmarks of this elegant style with its extra-long finish.

Whites between £10 and £12

Château Coucheroy AC Pessac-Léognan 93 13
(Febvre) *Wine merchants/off licences*
Soft acidity but fruit is there right through to the end.

★★ **Château de Rochemorin Andre Lurton AC Pessac-Léognan 93** 16
(Febvre) *Wine merchants/off licences*
Worth the extra cost for that special occasion. This wine just sings its way through to the last swallow. Citrus fruits with near perfect use of oak from a top winemaker make for a memorable drink.

White between £12 and £15

Château Doisy Daëne AC Bordeaux 93   13
(Mackenway)   *Wine merchants/off licences*
Offers really pleasant drinking with good fruit and
enough acidity to add a lively touch. Look for the most
recent vintage.

RED WINES

Red under £4.50

Borie-Manoux Claret AC Bordeaux nv   12
Dunnes Stores
Has the fruit and enough structure to make it a good
partner with food.

Reds between £5.25 and £6.50

Château Haut-Bignon AC Bordeaux 92   12
(Greenhills)   *Wine merchants/off licences*
Light in colour with a stalky rather than fruity flavour.

Château le Retou Alexis Lichine AC Bordeaux 92   12
(Greenhills)   *Widely available*
Reasonable quality for 92 with hints of liquorice and
stalky fruit.

Château les Tuileries AC Bordeaux Supérieur 89   13
(Remy)   *Wine merchants/off licences*
Everyday drinking. A big fruity and assertive vintage.

Château Michaud Alexis Lichine AC Bordeaux 92   12
(Greenhills)   *Widely available*
An example of the lighter style of the 92 vintage with
hints of brambly fruit.

Domaine du Moulin de Mendoce AC Côtes de Bourg 93
13
Quinnsworth
Earthy, with good Bordeaux character overlain with hints
of liquorice.

Premier de Lichine AC Bordeaux 92   13
(Greenhills)   *Widely available*
Brambly fruit with soft tannins. Pleasant drinking—
good with food.

Reds between £6.50 and £8

Alexis Lichine AC St Emilion 92   14
(Greenhills)   *Widely available*
Not a bad choice for 1992. An appealing whiff of
tobacco and good grip on the finish add interest.

B & G AC Bordeaux 90   13
(Dillons)   *Widely available*
Burnt smoky oak nose which appeals to the claret
drinker. Good blackberry fruit and supple tannins.

B & G Fondation 1725 AC Bordeaux 91   13
(Dillons)   *Widely available*
Very dependable in style with a consistently pleasing
quality. Rich in fruit with an easy supple finish.

Borie-Manoux AC Pauillac 93   14
                                    Dunnes Stores
A touch of tobacco aroma combines with good earthy
tones to make an interesting wine.

Calvet AC St Emilion 93   13
(Grants)   *Widely available*
Holds appeal in an easy-to-drink supple style. Just
enough 'bite' on the end to add interest.

Calvet Réserve AC Bordeaux 93   13
(Grants)   *Wine merchants/off licences*
Flows easily on the palate with the fruit lingering on the
finish. Consistent in style with hints of vanilla on the
finish.

PREMIER DE LICHINE

A.C. Bordeaux 1992
No 1 for Quality
No 1 for Value

The full range of Alexis Lichine French Wines
is imported and distributed solely by
Greenhills Wines and Spirits, Greenhills Road,
Walkinstown Dublin 12
Tel (01) 450 2178/9

Chai de Bordes-Quancard AC Bordeaux 93   13
(Brangan)   *Wine merchants/off licences*
Good example of basic Bordeaux. Garnet colour with
herbaceous fruit tones and a nice bite of tannin on the
finish.

Château Bechereau AC Bordeaux Supérieur 90   13
(MacCormaic)   *Wine merchants/off licences*
Tile brick in colour with herbaceous fruit tones. Some
bouquet development. Good example of a claret style at
this price level.

Château Bellevue Cru Bourgeois AC Médoc 93   13
                                          Quinnsworth
Purple toned with stalky fruits and a savoury extract.
Still young, with fruit and tannin fighting for first place.

Château Blaignan Cru Bourgeois AC Médoc 90   13
(Grants)   *Wine merchants/off licences*
Plenty of character with good texture and enough length
to add interest.

Château de Rabouchet AC Bordeaux 92   14
(Jenkinson)   *Wine merchants/off licences*
Intense ruby in colour. Firm tannins with hints of cedar
and subtle oak influence on the finish.

Château Holden AC Haut-Médoc 93   12
                                          Quinnsworth
Good body and structure with enough fruit to add
interest.

Château la Croix de Millorit AC Côtes de Bourg 90   13
                                          Quinnsworth
Cherry black in colour. Still young with fruit waiting to
emerge. A wine with potential. Needs food.

Château Labrie AC St Emilion 92   12
                                          Mitchells
Typical woodland aromas with mature brick colour.

Drinking well now.

Château le Boscq AC Médoc 93   14
Quinnsworth
A bite of fruit with a slightly astringent finish. Good food wine.

Château le Grand Verdus AC Bordeaux Supérieur 93   13
Quinnsworth
Closed on the nose but a very good example of the 93 vintage. Good concentrated fruit backed up with classic structure.

Château Timberlay AC Bordeaux Supérieur 92   14
(James Adams)   *Wine merchants/off licences*
Big and bold with generous ripe cassis fruit and good tannic grip.

Cordier Claret AC Bordeaux 92   13
(United Beverages)   *Wine merchants/off licences*
From a very reliable producer. Good colour and tightly knit fruit with good acidity and balance.

Croix de Margaux AC Margaux 92   13
Dunnes Stores
Not bad drinking for a 92. Soft plummy fruits with a slight earthy edge.

Dourthe AC Bordeaux 90   12
(Woodford Bourne)   *Wine merchants/off licences*
A decent everday drinking wine—uncomplicated but fruity and well made.

La Cour Pavillon AC Bordeaux 93   12
(Gilbeys)   *Widely available*
Everyday drinking—soft and easy with some length on the medium finish.

Michel Lynch AC Bordeaux 93   13
(Barry & Fitzwilliam)   *Widely available*

Still young but showing attractive hints of spice and cassis. Pleasant firm finish makes it a good food wine.

Mitchell & Son Claret AC Bordeaux 90   12
Mitchells

A good attack of sweet fruit is followed closely by drying tannins, making it a good food wine.

Mouton Cadet AC Bordeaux 90   12
(Findlaters)   *Widely available*

Tile brick in colour with rich cassis fruit and supple finish.

Sirius AC Bordeaux 90   14
(Fitzgeralds)   *Wine merchants/off licences*

Heady liquorice overtones. Deep ruby in colour. Classic claret structure at a fair price.

Reds between £8 and £10

B & G AC Margaux 90   13
(Dillons)   *Wine merchants/off licences*

Easy to drink with good fruit cake appeal and medium length.

Château Bel Air AC Bordeaux 93   13
Findlaters

Note the supple tannins and good bite of acidity on the long flavoursome finish.

Château Bonnet André Lurton AC Bordeaux 92   14
(Febvre)   *Wine merchants/off licences*

Another best buy of 92. Concentrated aromas overlain with toasty oak combine to give an elegant finish.

Château Cadillac Lesgourgues AC Bordeaux Supérieur 92
14
Mitchells

Deeply coloured. Good structure is followed by plenty of blackcurrant fruit and smooth tannins.

Château Canada AC Bordeaux Supérieur 91   13
Ecock   *Widely available*
Definite hints of chocolate and nutmeg. Mildly tannic
with a solid finish.

Château Cazebonne AC Graves 90   14
(Moore)   *Wine merchants/off licences*
Good example of Graves with strong earthy tones,
classic structure full of ripe red fruit flavours. Very
chunky—needs time.

**Château de Paillet-Quancard AC Premières Côtes de
Bordeaux 91**   12
(Brangan)   *Wine merchants/off licences*
Very pleasant aromas of woodland undergrowth which
carry through on flavour. Good balancing acidity and
tannin.

Château Dillon AC Haut-Médoc 93   14
                                        Quinnsworth
Wonderful aroma of cassis fruit overlain with a herbaceous bite. Classy claret flavours at a fair price.

Château la Rose Blanche Borie-Manoux AC St Emilion 90
                    Dunnes Stores   14
Baked fruit tones with a slight mineral character and
supple tannins.

Château Lagrange AC Lussac St Emilion 93   13
(Taserra)   *Wine merchants/off licences*
Pale in colour with soft fruits and supple tannins. Enjoy
now.

★**Château Lalande AC St Julien 93**   15
                    Dunnes Stores
Wonderful deep ruby in colour. Stalky brambly fruit
tones. Still young but already showing its fine potential.

★★ **Château le Bonnat AC Graves 93**   16
Quinnsworth

Top example of Graves offering superb taste at a great price. Good fruit and texture with that slight earthy finish so marked in Graves.

★ **Château Loudenne Cru Grand Bourgeois AC Médoc 90**
(Gilbeys)   *Widely available*   15
A good example of Médoc. Still 'closed' but it has the big structure of the 90 vintage with solid fruit waiting to re-emerge through the drying tannins.

Château Meaume AC Bordeaux Supérieur 92   12
(Findlaters)   *Wine merchants/off licences*
Deep ruby in colour with firm fruit and tannin.

★ **Château Moncets AC Lalande de Pomerol 90**   15
Searsons

Very attractive Merlot fruit style full of woodland, fig and fungi aromas, ending in a strong finish.

★ **Château Patache d'Aux Cru Bourgeois AC Médoc 93** 15
Quinnsworth

Shows what can be done in a less than perfect vintage. Quite an earthy style with good colour saturation, firm structure and a long finish.

Château Pichon AC Lussac St Emilion 93   12
(Taserra)   *Wine merchants/off licences*
Surprisingly light in style. Vegetal tones with high acidity and some hint of tannin.

Château Prieure Blaignan Cru Bourgeois AC Médoc 92 14
(Febvre)   *Wine merchants/off licences*
Choose the 92 vintage carefully. This certainly won't disappoint. Full of cedar tones, good cassis flavour and supple tannins.

Château Puyfromage AC Bordeaux Supérieur 92   12
(Brangan)   *Widely available*
Bitter-sweet on the finish. Good garnet colours with
supple tannins.

Château Sigognac Cru Bourgeois Médoc 90   14
(MacCormaic)   *Wine merchants/off licences*
Packed with fruit and just a hint of cinnamon. Good
balancing tannin and long finish.

Château Suau AC Premières Côtes de Bordeaux 89   12
(Moore)   *Widely available*
Nice classy claret with stalky fruit overtones.

Couvent de l'Eglise AC Pomerol 92   12
                                               Dunnes Stores
Easy-drinking style with some ripe fruit and an opulent
finish.

Domaine du Balardin AC Bordeaux Supérieur 90   11
(Febvre)   *Wine merchants/off licences*
With its smooth tannins, will appeal to those who like a
'soft' wine.

Le Clocher de St Julien AC St Julien 92   12
                                               Dunnes Stores
Young cherry aromas with youthful tannins and
balancing acidity. Easy drinking.

Reds between £10 and £12

B & G AC St Emilion 92   12
(Dillons)   *Widely available*
Straightforward St Emilion. Rich crimson colour, red
berry fruit appeal overlain with smoke.

Château Beaumont AC Haut-Médoc 89   13
                                               Searsons
Easy to drink, quite jammy in style but with enough
tannin to give structure.

Château Brown Alexis Lichine AC Pessac-Léognan 88 14
(Greenhills) *Widely available*
Drinking well now. Balanced with good cassis fruit,
medium acidity and balanced tannins.

★ **Château Camensac Cru Classé Haut-Médoc 89** 15
Searsons
Shows an exciting balance of mature flavours of stewed
prunes with a long concentrated finish.

Château de Sours AC Bordeaux Supérieur 90 14
Mitchells
So easy to enjoy with its good ripe fruit tones, velvet
texture and just enough tannin to give 'grip'.

Château Gaudet-Plaisance AC Montagne St Emilion 89 14
(Brangan) *Wine merchants/off licences*
From one of the surrounding satellite towns of St
Emilion. Benchmark style, with typical wood smoke
overtones.

★ **Château Haut Piquat AC Lussac St Emilion 90** 15
(Febvre) *Wine merchants/off licences*
All the hallmarks of good Merlot fruit are stamped on
this wine. Woodland aromas with excellent length and
an attractive rich fruit cake finish.

Château le Logis de Sipian AC Médoc 89 14
(Taserra) *Wine merchants/off licences*
Even though a little closed in the nose, voluptuous ripe
fruits on the palate are cut through with harmonious
tannins. A good example of the ripe 89 vintage which
will continue to mature for some time.

Château Magnol Cru Bourgeois AC Haut-Médoc 88 14
(Dillons) *Widely available*
Very appealing in a silky elegant style. Good length of
flavour. Rich and smooth.

MOËT & CHANDON

Fondé en 1743

Nederburg

Barton & Guestier

La passion du vin depuis 1725

Depuis 1731

BOUCHARD PÈRE & FILS

I.L. RUFFINO

CONTI SERRISTORI

BLUE NUN®

PAUL MASSON

SINCE 1852

BOLLA

SANDEMAN

EST 1790

MATEUS®

PRODUCED AND BOTTLED IN PORTUGAL

FOUNDED IN 1850

CARMEN

FONTANA CANDIDA

MONTECILLO

Fine wines from Edward Dillon.

★ **Château Millet AC Graves 90**   15
(Gilbeys)   *Wine merchants/off licences*
A fine example of red Graves with its earthy tones of
cedar and leather. Concentrated fruit extract combines
with firm tannins to give structure and class.

★ **Château Ramage la Batisse Cru Bourgeois AC Haut-
Médoc 90**   15
                                                                   Best Cellars
Straight away the ruby colour attracts. This follows
through on aroma with blackcurrant and oak tones.
Well balanced with an attractive savoury finish.

Haut Luccius Oak-aged AC Lussac St Emilion 90   12
(Taserra)   *Wine merchants/off licences*
Tile brick in colour with hints of liquorice and pleasant
woodland aroma. Drinking well at present.

La Bastide Dauzac Andre Lurton AC Margaux 92   14
(Febvre)   *Wine merchants/off licences*
Good depth of ripe red berry fruits and a dash of tannin
on the finish.

Reds between £12 and £15

Château Canon-Moueix AC Canon-Fronsac 89   13
                                                                    Searsons
Very dense in colour with strong plummy flavours
overlain with an earthy tone.

★ **Château de Cantin Cru Classé St Emilion 89**   15
(Moore)   *Wine merchants/off licences*
Brick tile in colour. Big, bold and delicious and a good
example of the opulent ripe 89 vintage.

★★ **Château de France AC Pessac-Léognan 89**   16
(Jenkinson)   *Wine merchants/off licences*
This wine has it all! Richly concentrated with mature
berry fruits, firm tannins and subtle oak.

★ **Château Haut-Logat Cru Bourgeois AC Haut-Médoc 90**   15
(Brangan)   *Wine merchants/off licences*
Dense colour and complex cedary tones. The tannins are
rich and ripe. Nice length to the finish.

Château la Tour de By Cru Bourgeois AC Médoc 90   14
(Mackenway)   *Wine merchants/off licences*
Ripe, plump and generous with complex fruit flavours.

Château Lamarque Cru Bourgeois AC Haut-Médoc 86
                  Mitchells   13
Robust in a muscular style with plenty of drying tannins
but ripe fruit is trying to break through.

**Château Lamothe-Bergeron Cru Bourgeois AC Haut-
Médoc 85**   14
(Febvre)   *Wine merchants/off licences*
Crimson with bouquet development of concentrated
cassis and wood smoke. Good ripe fruits with marked
length of flavour.

**Château Lanessan Cru Bourgeois Exceptionnel AC
Haut-Médoc 90**   14
(Grants)   *Wine merchants/off licences*
A robust wine with savoury fruit flavours and long finish.

★ **Château Pavie Grand Cru Classé St Emilion 90**   15
                                        Searsons
Another top example from a super vintage. It has all the
woodland smoke and damp forest tones that are the
hallmarks of good St Emilion.

Château Tayac Cru Bourgeois AC Margaux 90   14
(Gilbeys)   *Wine merchants/off licences*
Very appealing with its silky texture and ripe fruit tones.

Château Tour St Bonnet Cru Bourgeois AC Médoc 88   13
(Mackenway)   *Wine merchants/off licences*
Delivers both on fruit and style. Good concentration and
medium length.

Reds between £15 and £20

★ **Château Batailley 5ème Cru Classé Pauillac 91**   16
(Cassidy)   *Wine merchants/off licences*
For a 91 vintage this was stunning. Mocha floods the
palate with layer upon layer of ripe fruits. Tannin hits
the end but is supple and harmonious. A rich concentrated wine.

★ **Château Clarke Baron Ed. de Rothschild Cru Bourgeois
AC Listrac-Médoc 89**   15
(Brangan)   *Wine merchants/off licences*
Has the promise of Pauillac with its lovely cassis/gorse
nose, followed by good depth of flavour with harmonious tannin and balanced acidity. Smack of chocolate on
the finish.

★ **Château la Grange Grand Cru Classé St Julien 89**   15
Quinnsworth
Excellent introduction to classic Bordeaux. Chocolate
and nutmeg overtones with a big attack of ripe fruits
and flavours. An opulent classic wine at a fair price.

★ **Château Labégorce Cru Bourgeois AC Margaux 88**   15
Findlaters
Rich and full with fruit and tannin competing with each
other for first place. Well-developed fruit flavours win.
Extra-long finish.

Château Lapelletrie Cru Classé St Emilion 90   13
(Febvre)   *Wine merchants/off licences*
Fruit cake aromas and flavours lingering on make this a
good example of Merlot.

★ **Château Larosé Perganson Cru Bourgeois AC Médoc 89**
(Callaghan)   *Wine merchants/off licences*   15
Superb drinking. Deep crimson in colour. Attractive
supple style with plenty of brambly fruits and a hint of
oak.

★**Château Lynch Moussas 5ème Cru Classé Pauillac 91** 15
(Cassidy)   *Wine merchants/off licences*
A big wine in every sense. Rich concentrated aromas
and flavours with drying tannins and tight-knit fruit.

★**Château Mazeris AC Canon-Fronsac 89** 15
(Woodford Bourne)   *Wine merchants/off licences*
89 was a luscious vintage with rich fruit. This wine has
good depth of flavour and structure, finishing in a slight
earthy tone characteristic of the appellation.

★ **Château Smith Haut-Lafitte Grand Cru Classé Pessac-
Léognan/Graves 90** 16
Mitchells
Another stunner. More muscular in style but fruit fights
the tannin and holds great appeal.

Château Trimoulet Grand Cru Classé St Emilion 90 14
(Febvre)   *Wine merchants/off licences*
Smoky, damp forest appeal with red berry fruits coming
through on the finish.

Reds between £20 and £30

★★**Chateau de Fieuzal Cru Classé Pessac-Léognan 89** 16
Searsons
So appealing with its distinct earthy tone needing time
to open up. Generous in flavour and length.

★**Château Haut Bages Averous (2nd wine of Château
Lynch-Bages) AC Pauillac 88** 15
(Barry & Fitzwilliam)   *Wine merchants/off licences*
Rich and sturdy with the hallmarks of classic
winemaking. Offers good drinking at an affordable
price.

★**Château Kirwan 3ème Cru Classé Margaux 90** 16
(Remy)   *Wine merchants/off licences*
Another superb wine that is approachable now but will
benefit from further ageing. Silky smooth and balanced.

★ **Château la Grange Grand Cru Classé St Julien 85**   15
Quinnsworth

Another classic with mature complex tones. Very balanced oak with lots of pushing and shoving between fruit and tannin. Just note the oak on the very end of the delicious finish.

★ **Château la Lagune 3ème Cru Classé Haut-Médoc 85**   15
(Remy)   *Wine merchants/off licences*

Stands out from the wine crowd with its intense concentration and vanilla tones. Fans out in fruity layers and lingers long after the last swallow.

★★★**Château la Louvière AC Pessac-Léognan 88**   17
(Febvre)   *Wine merchants/off licences*

Never classified, this wine is rated by experts to be one of the tops. It's all in the taste with delicious ripe fruit and a soft velvet texture combining to give great length of flavour. Great vintage.

Château la Mouline de Labégorce AC Haut-Médoc 89   14
Findlaters

Big and savoury with good attack of fruit and spicy tones. Rich finish.

★★ **Château Langoa-Barton 3ème Cru Classé St Julien 86**   16
(Dillons)   *Wine merchants/off licences*

Often considered the most luscious of the Médoc appellations, this is a good example. Packed tight with masses of cassis fruit, excellent balance of oak and supple tannins.

★ **Château Lascombes Cru Classé Margaux 88**   15
(Greenhills)   *Wine merchants/off licences*

Classic Margaux. Smooth and silky. The 88 vintage takes time to come round, so note the touch of austerity in the finish, indicating that this hasn't peaked.

★★ **Château Leoville Barton 2ème Cru Classé St Julien 86**   17
(Dillons)   *Wine merchants/off licences*
Powerful with very concentrated fruit flavours wrapped
around rich tannins. Rich complex finish.

★ **Château Malescot St Exupery 3ème Grand Cru Classé
Margaux 89**   15
(Febvre)   *Wine merchants/off licences*
Classy Margaux with superb structure and balance
between fruit, tannin and acidity.

Château Soutard Grand Cru Classé St Emilion 89   14
(Mackenway)   *Wine merchants/off licences*
Mushrooms and blackcurrants—let your imagination
work overtime but above all just enjoy the drink.

★★ **Château Talbot 4ème Cru Classé St Julien 88**   16
(United Beverages)   *Wine merchants/off licences*
Packs a punch with rich powerful plummy tones
overlain with a hint of liquorice. Appealing long finish

Reds between £30 and £50

★★ **Château Cheval Blanc 1er Cru Classé 'A' St Emilion 87**   17
                                                       Searsons
Top estates usually produce top quality even in poor
years. This 87 has complex fruit and liquorice tones with
layers and layers of concentration. Enjoy it now. It
makes delicious drinking. Serve just below room
temperature. Wonderful!

★★ **Château Giscours 3ème Cru Classé Margaux 85**   16
(Grants)   *Wine merchants/off licences*
Rich and powerful with extraordinary balance between
the fruit, tannin and acidity. A wine to meditate over.

★★ **Château Lynch-Bages 5ème Cru Classé Pauillac 86**   17
(Barry & Fitzwilliam)   *Wine merchants/off licences*
Packed with exotic coffee, tobacco and herb aromas.
Concentrated powerful tannins needing time to harmo-
nise with fruit. A big and powerful wine.

[105   ]

★★★ **Château Palmer 3ème Cru Classé Margaux 92**   17

Searsons

A very classic style with aromas of woodland smoke, cedar and blackcurrant. On the palate the tannins are velvet soft and cut through by balancing acidity, leaving an impression of power and finesse. A fruit-driven classic.

★★★ **Château Trottevieille 1er Grand Cru Classé St Emilion 89**   17

(Cassidy)   *Wine merchants/off licences*

Aromas of figs with liquorice and leather tones. Intense, with good structure. The fruit flavour is all about liquorice but wait for the big attack of sweet fruits which follows. Velvet in texture.

ROSÉ WINES

Rosés between £6.50 and £8

Château de la Jaubertie AC Bergerac 94   12

Mitchells

Strawberry-tinted. Much more fruity on the palate than on the aroma. Slight hint of spritz—drink cool and fresh.

★ **Château Thieuley AC Bordeaux 94**   15

Wines Direct

Top-class Bordeaux rosé with pleasant strawberry colour and flavour. Good crisp acidity leaves a fresh finish.

Burgundy

Located in eastern France, Burgundy stretches from the town of Dijon in the north to Lyon in the south. It is a long, narrow strip of land which includes Chablis, the Côte d'Or (Golden Slope), comprising the Côte de Nuits and the Côte de Beaune, and, further south, the regions of Côte Chalonnaise, Mâconnais and Beaujolais.

Unlike Bordeaux, where there are large individual châteaux, Burgundy vineyards are very fragmented. Originally Church-owned, the vineyards were sold off after the French Revolution. Since that time, Napoleonic inheritance laws, which treat each child equally, have resulted in vineyards becoming smaller and smaller. Clos de Vougeot is often cited as an example. The vineyard, an area of 50 hectares, has over seventy separate owners, each owning a smallholding or plot of vines, making a patchwork of tiny plots. The end result is wines carrying the same appellation, but of variable quality. This is why it is important to get to know the wines of individual winemakers, négociants or merchants.

It could be argued that the original proponent of varietal wines was Burgundy. For centuries wine has been made from single grape varieties. Pinot Noir is the red grape, Chardonnay the white. Pinot Noir can lose its colour quite quickly, turning to 'brick'. The wines can be wonderfully aromatic, with a characteristic bite of ripe fruit and good acidity. Chardonnay styles vary from the steely bone dry of Chablis to the buttery-fat rich wines with oak influence of the Côte de Beaune. The Gamay produces Beaujolais, and lesser-known grape varieties include the white Bourgogne Aligoté, traditionally used in Kir. Red Burgundy was always known for its big, full-bodied wines, but in the past wines for export have been blended with north African or Rhône wines to bulk them out. Over the past twenty years, however, fashion has favoured purer wines.

Some terms explained

Mise en bouteille au domaine: Indicates a wine that has been made and bottled at the particular domaine.

Hospice de Beaune: Established in the town of the same name in 1443 to take care of the aged, infirm and poor of Beaune. The Hospice owns over 55 hectares of Premier and Grand Cru Beaune vineyards. Each year, on the third Sunday in November, these wines are sold by auction and usually set the price for other Burgundian wines of the year.

Négociant or *négociant-éleveur:* Négociant houses in Burgundy have existed for hundreds of years. The vast majority of them are located in Beaune and Nuits-St-Georges. These wine merchants handle much of the wine trade, buying in wine from growers and maturing, bottling and marketing it. Many also own vineyards.

Houses represented on the Irish market include Bichot, Bouchard Père et Fils, Lupé-Cholet, Delaunay, Joseph Drouhin, Domaine Dujac, Faiveley, Louis Jadot, Jaffelin, Laroche, Louis Latour, Mommessin, Moreau et Fils and Antonin Rodet—all highly recommended. Other merchant names offering good-value wines include Labouré-Roi, Marcilly, Pierre Ponnelle and Charles Viénot.

Classification

Basic appellations: Bourgogne Rouge, Bourgogne Blanc, Bourgogne Aligoté are on the bottom rung of the quality ladder. They are followed by *district appellations*, e.g. Beaujolais, Côte de Beaune, Côte de Nuits, Chablis. Next come the *communal appellations* such as Meursault or Pommard. Wines are blended from vineyards within the particular communal appellation. Vineyards within the village can prefix their name to the village AC in small print. These are known as 'lieux-dits'. Moving up in quality, next are the *Premier Cru* wines. Usually in the same-size lettering, the commune name is followed by the name of highly rated vineyard sites. Examples include wines such as Chambolle-Musigny Les Amoureuses, Aloxe-Corton Les Chaillots, Beaune Les Grèves, Pommard Les Epenots, Gevrey-Chambertin Les Gémeaux. To add confusion, communes have always had the right to use the name of their most famous vineyard. Therefore the top-growth Le Chambertin located in the commune of Gevrey becomes Gevrey-Chambertin. *Grand Cru:* Highest-quality Burgundian wine. Here the vineyard or plot of land itself is classified, e.g. Le Chambertin, La Tâche, Le Montrachet, Le Corton, Le Musigny. The majority of Grand Cru reds are located in the Côte de Nuits and the majority of white in the Côte de Beaune.

Burgundy appellations available in Ireland

Chablis: It is difficult to grow grapes this far north in France; spring frosts can annihilate an entire harvest practically overnight. Chablis covers a large appellation area and the wines fall into several quality categories. Most production is of straightforward Chablis AC. Next in quality are the seventeen Premier Cru vineyards such as Fourchaume, Montmains, Vaillons and Montée de Tonnerre. At the top of the tree are the seven Chablis Grands Crus, which are more complex. Worth remembering, they are Blanchots, Bougros, Les Clos, Grenouilles, Preuses, Valmur and Vaudésir.

Côte de Nuits: Lies in the northern half of the Côte d'Or. Production consists mainly of red wines, with some white being produced. Red wine appellations called after their communes include Fixin, Gevrey-Chambertin, Morey-St-Denis, Chambolle-Musigny, Vougeot, Flagey-Echézeaux, Vosne-Romanée, Nuits-St-Georges.

Côte de Beaune: Located in the southern part of the Côte d'Or. The best white wines of Burgundy come from here, with top-quality red wines also produced. Commune appellations include Savigny-lès-Beaune, Pernand-Vergelesses, Ladoix-Serrigny, Aloxe-Corton, Chorey-lès-

Beaune, Pommard, Volnay, Monthélie, Meursault, Puligny-Montrachet, Chassagne-Montrachet, Auxey-Duresses, St Romain, St Aubin, Santenay.

Côte Chalonnaise appellations include Givry, Mercurey (red wine predominates), Rully (red and white wine) and Montagny (white).

Mâconnais: Most white wine production centres on Chardonnay without oak influence. Wines are meant for early consumption. Appellations include Mâcon, Mâcon-Villages (43 villages can affix their name, including some of the most popular on the Irish market, such as Viré, Lugny, Loché and Vinzelles), Mâcon Supérieur and St Véran. The most famous white wine of the Mâconnais is Pouilly-Fuissé. The wine is quite a rich, usually high-alcohol, style of Chardonnay and boasts a large following. Fruity easy-drinking red wines are also produced here from the Gamay grape of Beaujolais fame. The same appellations of Mâcon, Mâcon with a village name and Mâcon Supérieur apply to the red wines.

Beaujolais: Thirty-four miles long and about nine miles across, the wine region of Beaujolais is located at the southern end of Burgundy. The red Gamay is used here, and thrives on the granite soil of the region. Most Beaujolais production is red, though a little white wine is produced. Straightforward Beaujolais is always best drunk in the year of its birth. Beaujolais-Villages wines have longer staying power and can be drunk up to three years after the vintage. Beaujolais Nouveau, or Beaujolais Primeur, released on the third Thursday in November, should be drunk in the months leading up to Christmas. This wine has declined greatly in popularity in recent years. The Crus come from the top villages located in the north of the region. Each Beaujolais Cru (of which there are ten) is distinguished by its own individual aromas and flavours. The ten Crus are Brouilly, Côte de Brouilly, Chénas, Chiroubles, Fleurie, Morgon, Moulin à Vent, Régnié, St Amour and Juliénas. All have the ability to age from two to fifteen years, depending on the vintage. If the wines are not up to the standard of their Cru they are declassified into simple Bourgogne, which automatically makes them very different in style to the Pinot Noir Bourgogne wines of the Côte Chalonnaise!

WHITE WINES

White under £4.50

Labouré-Roi AC St Véran 93 12
Quinnsworth
Pale in colour. Surprisingly fresh on the finish.

White between £5.25 and £6.50

Pierre Ponnelle AC Mâcon 94 13
Dunnes Stores
Deep lemon in colour. Apple fruit follows through on the palate leaving a clean fresh finish.

Whites between £6.50 and £8

Alexis Lichine AC Mâcon-Villages 93 12
(Greenhills) *Wine merchants/off licences*
Straightforward easy drink with a slight earthy tone.

Cave de Lugny Les Charmes AC Mâcon-Lugny 93 13
(Mackenway) *Wine merchants/off licences*
Subtle hints of peach, good weight of fruit and a long balanced finish.

★ **Charles Viénot AC Rully 93** 15
Superquinn
Top example of this appellation. Pale lemon in colour with a hint of oak influence. Good balancing acidity and some length to finish.

Delaunay et Fils Sauvignon de St Bris VDQS 93 12
(Brangan) *Wine merchants/off licences*
Pleasant mineral tones with good attack of fruit and acidity. Some hint of apple on the end.

Dominique Piron Chardonnay AC Mâcon 93   13
(Barry & Fitzwilliam)   *Widely available*
Hints of peachy fruit. Blancing acidity gives a fresh
finish.

Labouré-Roi AC Montagny 92   13
    Quinnsworth
Deep golden in colour. Hints of ripe peach. Good acidity
and fruit attack. Good quality/price ratio.

Labouré-Roi Chardonnay AC Bourgogne 94   12
    Quinnsworth
Good yellow tones with nutty flavour in an easy-to-drink
style.

Les Genievres AC Mâcon-Lugny 93   13
(Gilbeys)   *Widely available*
Well-made Mâcon with good balance of peachy tones
cut through by fresh acidity.

Les Vignerons d'lgé AC Mâcon-Villages 93   13
(Febvre)   *Widely available*
Fragrance of peach with nice soft fruits and medium
length on the finish.

Whites between £8 and £10

Alexis Lichine AC Chablis 94   13
(Greenhills)   *Widely available*
Good balance of fruit and acidity, but short on the
finish.

Bouchard Père et Fils AC Bourgogne Aligoté 93   14
(Dillons)   *Widely available*
Dominated by greengage fruit, an arrow of crisp acid
leaves the palate fresh and clean. Use with two tea-
spoonfuls of Crème de Cassis to make Kir.

Bouchard Père et Fils AC Mâcon-Villages 93   14
(Dillons)   *Widely available*

Dried apricot aromas with good balance of acidity and alcohol.

Faiveley AC Mâcon-Villages 92 12
(Remy) *Widely available*
Surprisingly deep colour. At three years old, the fruit was fading. Younger vintages are full of freshness with a lively finish.

J. Moreau et Fils AC Chablis 93 14
(Grants) *Wine merchants/off licences*
Steely tone without any hint of oak. Good refreshing acidity is cut through with greengage fruits. Good value.

Labouré-Roi AC Pouilly-Fuissé 94 13
Quinnsworth
Very pale with hints of green. Better on the palate, with good attack, initial crisp acidity and some length to finish.

Laroche AC Mâcon-Lugny 93 14
(Allied Drinks) *Widely available*
Deep gold in colour with hints of peach. Clean and fresh in style with good length.

Louis Latour Les Genievres AC Mâcon-Lugny 93 14
(Gilbeys) *Widely available*
Elegant with all the hallmarks of well-made Chardonnay without oak influence—enjoy it young.

William Fèvre VDQS Sauvignon de St Bris 93 13
(Febvre) *Wine merchants/off licences*
Will appeal to those who like lemon-type acidity. Zesty and crisp. Good attack and pronounced length to finish.

Whites between £10 and £12

Charles Viénot AC Meursault 92 13
Superquinn
Very appealing with its toasty hazelnuts and an elegant, long finish.

★ **Château de Rully Domaine Comtes C. de Ternay AC Rully 93** 15
(Febvre) *Widely available*
A perfect example of the top-quality white wines being produced further south in Burgundy. It has rich fruit, buttery overtones and a long smooth finish.

J. Moreau et Fils AC Pouilly-Fuissé 93 14
(Grants) *Widely available*
Blackberry leaf aromas with a good attack of fruit that ends in a lingering yet subtle finish.

Jean Marc Brocard Domaine Ste Claire AC Chablis 93 13
(Moore) *Wine merchants/off licences*
Enough racy acidity and mineral overtones to enjoy now or keep for a couple more years.

Joseph Drouhin AC Rully 93 13
(Searsons) *Widely available*
Good Chardonnay fruit and balanced elegant finish.

La Chablisienne AC Chablis 93 14
(Mackenway) *Wine merchants/off licences*
A vigorous wine. Note the pale colour, clean apple-type fruit and stamp of acidity.

★ **Laroche AC Chablis 93** 15
(Allied Drinks) *Widely available*
Dry with a streak of steely acidity counterbalanced with apple-type fruit.

Les Chagnots Antonin Rodet 1er Cru Montagny 93 13
(Febvre) *Wine merchants/off licences*
Nutty tones, very subtle and elegant, which continue on flavour and finish on a high note.

★**Louis Latour AC Chablis 94**   15
(Gilbeys)   *Wine merchants/off licences*
Has it all—the steely mineral tone with crisp acidity and
good length on the finish.

Louis Latour AC Puligny-Montrachet 93   14
(Gilbeys)   *Wine merchants/off licences*
Pale in colour. Delicate aromas with an unmistakably
nutty tone. Fruit and hazelnuts mingle on the palate.

Montagny Prosper Manfoux 1er Cru Montagny 92   12
(Mitchells)   *Wine merchants/off licences*
Pale in colour with hints of biscuity tones. A good attack
of fruit develops and ends in a medium finish.

Regnard AC Chablis 92   13
(Gilbeys)   *Wine merchants/off licences*
Nutty and toasty with all the hallmarks of good cool
climate Chardonnay. Finishes well with tangy acidity.

Whites between £12 and £15

Alain Geoffroy Fourchaume 1er Cru Chablis 93   14
(Febvre)   *Widely available*
Flavours of apple and a touch of biscuit fan out and
leave a lingering finish—an example of good
winemaking.

Bouchard Ainé AC Chablis 94   13
(Cassidy)   *Wine merchants/off licences*
Sharp arrow of acidity cuts through the nutty fruit
tones.

Delaunay Vaillons 1er Cru Chablis 94   14
(Brangan)   *Widely available*
Still young. Flinty stony tone of good Chablis with fruit
fanning out on the palate and acidity kicking back on
the finish.

★ **Domaine Bois-Seguin 1er Cru Chablis 93** 15
(Searsons) *Widely available*
Top-class Chablis shot through with crisp acidity and a
bone dry clean finish.

La Chablisienne Fourchaume 1er Cru Chablis 93 13
(Mackenway) *Widely available*
Lingering apple flavours—toasted bread on the finish
makes interesting drinking.

Louis Michel AC Chablis 94 14
(Findlaters) *Widely available*
Benchmark Chablis with its mineral tones and pleasant
crisp clean flavours cut through with tingling acidity.

William Fèvre Fourchaume 1er Cru Chablis 94 14
(Febvre) *Wine merchants/off licences*
From one of the most respected and outspoken makers
of Chablis. Rich yet lean fruit with powerful balance and
satisfying length on the finish.

Whites between £15 and £20

★ **Cuvée Prestige Guy Moreau Vaillons 1er Cru Chablis
92** 15
(Grants) *Widely available*
Produced in honour of the winemaker's father, from 60-
year-old vines this wine is an example of subtle harmony
and elegance.

Jules Belin AC Meursault 93 12
(Febvre) *Widely available*
Has a touch of hazelnut with enough acidity and
lingering fruit to attract attention.

Labouré-Roi Poruzot AC Meursault 92 13
Quinnsworth
Has the stamp of hazelnuts associated with Meursault.
Good balancing acidity adds crispness to the finish.

★ **Louis Jadot AC Meursault 91** 15
(Grants) *Wine merchants/off licences*
Top quality with its rich buttery fruit and fresh acidity.
Balanced and elegant.

Pierre Ponnelle AC Puligny-Montrachet 92 14
Dunnes Stores
Subtle oaky tones. Melon and apple fruit flavours end in
a well-balanced refreshing toasty finish.

White between £20 and £30

★ **Domaine Pinson Les Clos Grand Cru Chablis 92** 15
(Callaghan) *Widely available*
All the hallmarks of quality, with its backbone of steely
acidity and slight nutty nuances.

RED WINES

Reds between £5.25 and £6.50

Charles Viénot AC Mâcon Supérieur 93 14
Superquinn
Deep crimson in colour with dense plummy tones. Good
structure with lots of up-front attack with enough acidity
to give balance. Well made. Great value/price
ratio.

Charles Viénot Pinot Noir AC Bourgogne 92 13
Superquinn
Fresh and tasty raspberry fruits, full of young tangy
Pinot Noir and acidity.

Reds between £6.50 and £8

Alexis Lichine AC Beaujolais-Villages 93 12
(Greenhills) *Wine merchants/off licences*
Pale in colour. Raspberry fruit flavours in an easy-
drinking style.

B & G St Louis AC Beaujolais 94   12
(Dillons)   *Wine merchants/off licences*
A fruity pleasant Beaujolais.

Domaine de Montgenas Fleurie Beaujolais Cru 94   12
                                              Quinnsworth
Lots of supple silky tones and an easy-drinking finish.

Georges Duboeuf AC Beaujolais-Villages 94   13
(James Adam)   *Wine merchants/off licences*
This name inspires confidence. The wine has the brilliant
ruby colour with all the zippy fruit, zesty acidity and
clean fresh finish one expects from this AC.

Labouré-Roi Pinot Noir AC Bourgogne 93   12
                                              Quinnsworth
Delicate Pinot characteristics carry through on flavour
with subtle tannins and some length to finish.

Les Burdelines Moulin à Vent Beaujolais Cru 93   14
                                              Quinnsworth
Big round and wonderful chewy fruit. Top quality at a
very fair price.

**Les Vignerons d'Igé AC Bourgogne Passetoutgrains
93/4**   12
(Febvre)   *Wine merchants/off licences*
Red berry fruit. Low in tannin with a bite of acidity to
add freshness. Serve cool to highlight the fruit.

Mommesin AC Mâcon Supérieur 93   13
                                                Mitchells
Plummy fruit development with a soft centre. A bite of
tannin and acidity adds interest to the finish.

Morgon le Clachet Beaujolais Cru 94   14
                                              Quinnsworth
Pronounced raspberry fruit aromas with enough
structure to give added interest.

Reds between £8 and £10

Bouchard Père et Fils AC Beaujolais-Villages 93   11
(Dillons)   *Wine merchants/off licences*
Easy-drinking with cherry fruits and medium long
finish.

Bouchard Père et Fils AC Mâcon Supérieur 94   11
(Dillons)   *Widely available*
Approachable uncomplicated style that delivers on red
berry fruits and finishes with crisp acidity.

★**Charles Viénot les Lavières 1er Cru Savigny-lès-
Beaune 92**   15
                                                              Superquinn
Deep crimson. Figs and chocolate nose. Hints of nutmeg.
Good attack of fruit fans out on the palate. Supple
tannins. Good length to finish.

Daniel Rion AC Bourgogne Passetoutgrains 90   13
(Brangan)   *Wine merchants/off licences*
Super fruit aromas and flavours. Long clean finish.

Faiveley Brouilly Beaujolais Cru 93   13
(Remy)   *Wine merchants/off licences*
Purple-toned with lots of balance between fruit, acidity
and supple tannins. Good long finish.

★**Georges Duboeuf Chiroubles Beaujolais Cru 94**   15
(James Adams)   *Wine merchants/off licences*
From the uncrowned King of Beaujolais. This wine
explains why. Well structured. Strawberry fruits.

Mommessin AC Côte de Beaune-Villages 90   13
                                                              Mitchells
Tile brick in colour. The wine has assumed the farmyard
characteristics of Pinot. Supple tannins, good fruit/
acidity balance.

Mommesin Morgon Beaujolais Cru 94 14
Mitchells
Lots of the cherry fruits associated with the Gamay
grape. Balanced tannins, acidity and structure add
quality.

Piat Père et Fils Fleurie Beaujolais Cru 94 14
(Gilbeys) *Widely available*
Consistent in style with elegance and charm. Good
underlying structure.

Reds between £10 and £12

Bouchard AC Hautes Côtes de Beaune 93 14
(Dillons) *Wine merchants/off licences*
Firm, flavoursome with raspberry fruits and a slight
touch of earthiness to the finish.

Bouchard AC Mercurey 90 14
(Dillons) *Widely available*
A rustic style. Good earthy fruit flavours with a shock of
high acidity and a long slightly spicy finish.

★ **Bouchard AC Savigny-lès-Beaune 90** 15
(Dillons) *Widely available*
A top example of Savigny-lès-Beaune. Well-rounded
supple texture, juicy strawberry fruit and firm finish.

Bouchard Aîné Fleurie Beaujolais Cru 93 12
(Cassidy) *Widely available*
Up-front strawberry flavours in an easy-drinking style.
Good structure but on the expensive side.

Bouchard Fleurie Beaujolais Cru 94 14
(Dillons) *Widely available*
A little pricey but worth it. Very appealing in style with
chunky fruits and good structure.

Domaine de la Tour du Bief Moulin à Vent Beaujolais Cru 94 13
(Taserra) *Widely available*
Deep purple/pink in colour with good structure and balance. Fresh raspberry fruits with a firm finish.

Georges Duboeuf Fleurie Beaujolais Cru 94 14
(James Adams) *Widely available*
Silky texture cut through with raspberry-like fruits. Enough tannin and acidity to give structure.

Labouré-Roi AC Nuits-St-Georges 91 13
Quinnsworth
A little delicate in mid-palate but good structure and sweet fruit attack. Easy-drinking style.

Les Bruyères Château de Chenas Moulin à Vent Beaujolais Cru 93 14
(Brangan) *Widely available*
Spicy, earthy. Typical chewy fruit expected from a top-class Beaujolais Cru.

Les Charmes au Châtelain AC Bourgogne 93 13
Burgundy Direct
Wonderful raspberry tones and an elegant structure.

Lupé Cholet AC Côte de Beaune-Villages 93 13
(Findlaters) *Superquinn*
Plummy in style. It has the fruit and just enough drying tannin to add structure.

Métrat et Fils Fleurie la Roilette Vieilles Vignes Beaujolais Cru 94 14
(Searsons) *Widely available*
Crimson in colour with very appealing raspberry fruits and a rich finish.

Robert Sarrau Château de St Amour Beaujolais Cru 93 12
(Taserra) *Widely available*

Pale in colour with light ripe raspberry tones, supple
tannins and medium finish.

Reds between £12 and £15

★ **Charles Viénot AC Nuits-St-Georges 90**   15
Superquinn

Super! Deep cherry in colour. Lots of opulence with ripe
fruit attack and characteristic Pinot farmyard nose.

★ **Château de Chamirey AC Mercurey 90**   15
(Febvre)   *Wine merchants/off licences*

Traditional fermentation with extended skin contact for
up to ten days and new oak maturation make a silky
supple wine with harmonious tannins and good fruit
appeal reminiscent of a Côtes de Beaune.

Château des Capitans Juliénas Beaujolais Cru 93   13
(Taserra)   *Wine merchants/off licences*

Wonderful cherry colour. Good bite of raspberry fruits
and acidity with just a hint of tannin. Drinking well
now.

Delaunay Clos l'Evèque 1er Cru Mercurey 91   14
(Brangan)   *Wine merchants/off licences*

From the Côte Chalonnaise in southern Burgundy. 91
was an uneven vintage but this wine has good intense
fruit with vibrant acidity and tannins that are softening
out.

★ **Domaine Besancenot AC Pernand Vergelesses 90**   15
Burgundy Direct

Mature complex aromas of farmyard and fruit tones.
Good attack. Flavours fan out and leave a rich long
finish.

Faiveley Clos des Myglands 1er Cru Mercurey 92   14
(Remy)   *Widely available*

Consistent in style, Faiveley produces super ripe
Mercurey wines with lots of sweet fruit, smooth tannins
and lingering flavours.

Labouré-Roi AC Pommard 91   14
Quinnsworth

Strawberry fruits with a good bite of balanced acidity and tannin. Silky texture and finish.

Louis Jadot AC Côte de Beaune-Villages 90   14
(Grants)   *Wine merchants/off licences*
Another benchmark Côte de Beaune. The 90 vintage was sunny and warm so expect lots of ripe fruit tones.

Mommessin AC Nuits-St-Georges 92   13
Mitchells

Better taste than aroma, with lots of spicy fruits and drying tannins. Medium body and structure.

★ **Pierre Ponnelle AC Gevrey-Chambertin 92**   15
Dunnes Stores

Young raspberry Pinot fruit. Well balanced with good acidity and fruit showing through subtle tannins.

> Reds between £15 and £20

★ **Delaunay AC Gevrey-Chambertin 88**   15
(Brangan)   *Wine merchants/off licences*
Ruby coloured with finesse and elegance. A huge attack of sweet fruit with an extra-smooth texture.

Joseph Drouhin AC Nuits-St-Georges 89   14
(Searsons)   *Wine merchants/off licences*
Classic style—big, bold, spicy and mature.

> Reds between £20 and £30

★★ **Domaine Besancenot Bressandes 1er Cru Beaune 90** 16
Burgundy Direct

Classic Pinot Noir. The promise of fruit on the nose imprints its impression on the palate. The wine's structure and weight are classic Burgundian. Delicious supple finish.

★ **Domaine Dujac AC Morey St Denis 90**   16
(Findlaters)   *Widely available*
Ignore the light saturation of colour and just zoom in on
the wonderful farmyard Pinot nose. Harmonious with
supple tannins and lots of sweet fruit attack.

★ **Faiveley Clos de la Maréchale 1er Cru Nuits-St-
Georges 88**   15
(Remy)   *Widely available*
88 was a muscular vintage. Bags of fruit hide behind
dense tannins, but the classic Pinot farmyard nose and
bite of acidity come through.

Louis Jadot AC Nuits-St-Georges 89   14
(Grants)   *Wine merchants/off licences*
Deep in colour and spicy tones. Good assertive long
finish.

★ **Michel Prunier Clos du Val 1er Cru AC Auxey-
Duresses 92**   16
(Callaghan)   *Widely available*
Wonderful drinking. Produced from 100% Pinot Noir.
Delicious raspberry fruit overlain with hints of cinnamon
and balanced acidity. Extra long flavour on finish.

Red between £30 and £50

★ **Domaine Dujac Aux Combottes 1er Cru Gevrey-
Chambertin 91**   17
Findlaters
Wonderful! Deep cherry in colour with a highly per-
fumed nose reminiscent of violets. Lots of spicy fruit
tones combine with supple tannins. Notice the pleasant
austere twist on the finish. A wine with great class.

Corsica

Located one hundred miles off the French Mediterranean coast, Corsica produces red, white, rosé, sparkling and sweet wines.

Classification

AC wines produced here are Ajaccio and Patrimonio (the best known). By the year 2000 Patrimonio must include 95% of the traditional red variety Nielluccio in the blend and 100% of Vermentino in white wine. Vin de Pays represents one-third of production, the best known being Vin de Pays de l'Île de Beauté.

Red between £5.25 and £6.50

'L' Laroche Pinot Noir VDP Ile de Beauté 93   12
(Allied Drinks)   *Widely available*
A nice easy-drinking wine with plenty of appeal, but not a typical Pinot Noir.

Loire

Located in the west and centre of France, the Loire region stretches along the river of the same name, which meanders through the region for over six hundred miles. The area can be broken into four distinct wine regions: Pays Nantes, Anjou-Saumur, Touraine and the Upper Loire.

A vast range of styles is produced, from dry whites needing years to mature to dry crisp early-drinking whites. Some of France's greatest dessert wines are produced here. The region is famous for dry and off-dry rosé wines. Red and sparkling wines are also made.

Loire wines available in Ireland

Pays Nantes
Muscadet: Named after the grape from which it is produced. There are several distinct appellations. One mentions the word *Muscadet* only. A second adds *de Sèvre-et-Maine*, indicating that the wine was produced within the areas of these two tributaries of the Loire river. Another is *Muscadet des Coteaux de la Loire*, seldom seen in Ireland. The words *sur lie* on the label indicate that the young wine was left on its own lees or sediment up to the time of bottling. This process helps enhance freshness and adds a slight yeasty or biscuity tone to the wine.

Gros Plant: Not often seen here, this VDQS is bone dry and once again named after the grape variety.

Anjou
Famed for its rosé wines, yet some interesting red wines are also being produced. White wine production is larger than red and ranges from dry to sweet.
Anjou Gamay: Red wine produced from the Gamay grape of Beaujolais fame.
Rosé d'Anjou: Medium-sweet rosé wine.
Cabernet d'Anjou: Sweet or dry.
Saumur: Red and white wines.

Saumur-Champigny: Fashionable red wine.

Sparkling Saumur: Large production of quality wine.

Savennières: This tiny area in the Anjou region produces some of the longest lived of all French white wines from the Chenin Blanc grape. Two sub-appellations, *Coulée de Serrant* and *La Roche-aux-Moines*, can mature for decades, assuming superb complexity with bottle age, but (be warned!) it takes years for the wines to lose their initial tart acidity.

Sweet wines: Bonnezeaux and Quarts de Chaume. Usually affected by noble rot, these are some of the most prized dessert wines of France, with great ageing ability.

Coteaux du Layon: A large area also producing sweet but much less complex wines from Chenin Blanc.

Touraine:

It is in Touraine that the red grape variety Cabernet Franc (known locally as 'le Breton') comes into its own. Particularly suited to this cooler climate, there are three major appellations covering the red wines. Named after individual towns, they are *Chinon, Bourgueil* and *St Nicolas de Bourgueil*. Although produced from the same grape variety, styles differ according to soil and vineyard location. Some of the best examples are from vines grown in the chalk-based soil known as tufa.

Red, white and rosé wines are produced.

Vouvray: Produced entirely from the Chenin Blanc grape (known locally as 'Pineau de la Loire'), this white wine can be dry, off-dry, sweet or sparkling. Not always indicated on the label, the degree of sweetness is described as *sec, demi-sec* and *molleux*.

Upper Loire

Sancerre: These vineyards, formally known as the Central vineyards of the Loire, produce the finest examples of zesty aromatic Sauvignon Blanc in France. The villages of *Sancerre* and *Pouilly sur Loire*, carrying their own appellations, are some of the best-known white wines of the area. Pouilly uses the word *fumé* to describe a natural white dust which settles on the underleaf of the vine. In windy weather, when viewed from a distance, it appears as smoke. Some people also claim to detect a distinct smokiness in the taste of the wine. Red and rosé Sancerre is produced from Pinot Noir. *Menetou-Salon:* White, red and rosé. Whites are produced from Sauvignon Blanc, reds and rosés from Pinot Noir. Other appellations not often seen in Ireland include *St Pourçain, Côtes du Forez, Quincy* and *Reuilly*.

WHITE WINES

Whites between £5.25 and £6.50

'L' Chardonnay Henri Laroche VDP Jardin de la France 93   12
(Allied Drinks)   *Widely available*
This Chardonnay without oak influence is all about green apples. Clean refreshing finish.

B & G AC Muscadet de Sèvre et Maine 93   12
(Dillons)   *Widely available*
Look for the most recent vintage. Should be dry with lively fruit and sometimes a hint of spritz.

Château de la Botinière AC Muscadet de Sèvre et Maine sur lie 94   13
                                    Quinnsworth
Green apple flavours. Slight spritzy tone and good lively acidity. Good choice for seafood.

Haut Poitou Sauvignon VDQS 94   13
(Gilbeys)   *Widely available*
Green apple flavours. Fresh and crisp with good length and zesty acidity. Reminiscent of Sancerre.

Marquis de Goulaine Chardonnay VDP Jardin de la France 93   13
(Gilbeys)   *Wine merchants/off licences*
Chalky mineral aroma. Apple flavour with the backbone of acidity associated with good Loire whites.

Whites between £6.50 and £8

Château de Goulaine AC Muscadet de Sèvre et Maine sur lie 94 12
(Gilbeys) *Widely available*
Has the bone dry finish of Muscadet with enough fruity extract and slight yeasty finish to add interest.

Château de la Cassemichère AC Muscadet de Sèvre et Maine sur lie 94 13
(Grants) *Widely available*
Fresh tangy apple fruits mix with yeasty overtones and ensure long flavour development.

Château du Cleray AC Muscadet de Sèvre et Maine sur lie 94 13
(James Adams) *Wine merchants/off licences*
Stony fruit tones follow through on taste with a hint of new baked bread on the finish.

Domaine de la Noë AC Muscadet de Sèvre et Maine sur lie 93 13
(Mackenway) *Wine merchants/off licences*
Its all here—the green apple fruits, tangy acidity and firm yet biscuity finish.

Whites between £8 and £10

★**Château de la Ragotière Cru AC Muscadet de Sèvre et Maine sur lie 93** 15
(Brangan) *Wine merchants/off licences*
White gold in colour with hints of Granny Smith apple. Shot through with a pleasant bite of acidity with fruit winning out on the long dry finish.

Château Moncontour AC 93 13
(Febvre) *Wine merchants/off licences*
Dry style with all the crispness backed up with apple fruits that one expects.

Wines
from the
Worlds Best Cellars

The proud traditions which emanate from Gilbeys date back to 1857 when Walter and Alfred Gilbey first sought to provide the very finest of wines to the gentry of the last century.

Now in 1995, Gilbeys reputation as an importer of fine wines from around the world is unsurpassed. Gilbeys has a long and proud tradition of delivering a wide variety of premium wines to the Irish consumer.

Come and explore the world of Gilbeys wines:

- **Hunters, New Zealand**
- **Faustino, Spain**
- **Santa Rita, Chile**
- **Jaboulet, Rhone**
- **De Ladoucette, Loire**
- **Drouhin, Burgundy**
- **Louis Latour, Alsace**
- **Laurent Perrier, Champagne**

Gilbeys of Ireland Ltd., Gilbey House, Belgard Road, Tallaght, Dublin 24.
Tel: (01) 459 7444. Fax: (01) 459 0188.

Domaine Couillaud Chardonnay VDP Jardin de la France 12
(Brangan) *Wine merchants/off licences*
Pleasant lean green fruits with balanced rounded acidity.

Le Master de Donatien AC Muscadet de Sèvre et Maine sur lie 93 14
(Woodford Bourne) *Widely available*
Pale in colour with a hint of spritz on the palate. Nice biscuit tones with good length.

Mark Brédif AC Vouvray 90 14
(Gilbeys) *Widely available*
The initial attack of greengage fruit is quickly overtaken by very crisp acidity. Good food wine.

Whites between £10 and £12

Château de Tracy AC Pouilly-Fumé 93 14
(Febvre) *Widely available*
Gooseberry aromas with a slight smokiness. crisp acidity cuts through the fruit. Finishes dry.

Domaine du Colombien AC Sancerre 93 13
(Brangan) *Wine merchants/off licences*
Lean stony fruit with that lactic overtone from lees contact. Dry clean finish with good depth of fruit.

Domaine Jean Paul Balland AC Sancerre 93 14
(Reynolds) *Widely available*
Reminiscent of tinned grapefruit with medium acidity and a medium finish.

★ **Domaine Vacheron AC Sancerre 94** 15
(Febvre) *Widely available*
Quality Sauvignon Blanc with hints of green in the colour. Fresh mown grass, gooseberry aromas and flavours with zingy acidity and good length on the finish.

Whites between £12 and £15

★ **Comte La Fond AC Sancerre 93** 15
(Gilbeys) *Widely available*
Good example of what Sancerre should be. Crisp fruity
gooseberry tones that dance on the palate and make one
reach for more.

★★ **de Ladoucette AC Pouilly-Fumé 92** 16
(Gilbeys) *Widely available*
Rich and elegant with pungent fruit tones and fresh
acidity. Elegant long finish.

★★ **Jean Max Roger AC Sancerre 94** 16
(Callaghan) *Wine merchants/off licences*
Top quality Sancerre with gooseberry aromas and
flavours. Tingling fresh acidity and crisp finish.

★ **Jolivet AC Pouilly Fumé 94** 15
(Brangan) *Wine merchants/off licences*
Superb elegant nose with ever-expanding fruit flavours
cut through with zesty acidity.

Whites between £30 and £50

Baron de 'L' AC Pouilly-Fumé 90 14
(Gilbeys) *Wine merchants/off licences*
Elegant but expensive. Has the classic subtle structure
with fruit breaking through the acidity.

★★ **Clos de la Coulée de Serrant AC Savennières 79** 16
(Searsons) *Wine merchants/off licences*
One of the finest wines in France, requiring years to
mature. A dry wine from the Chenin Blanc grape. It
assumes elegant richness as it matures. Buy young
vintages to lay down or, if you can afford it buy an older
one such as this.

RED WINES

Red between £6.50 and £8

Couly-Dutheil Les Gravières AC Chinon 93   12
(Gilbeys)   *Wine merchants/off licences*
Ruby red with pungent characteristic stalky-type fruit.

Red between £8 and £10

Château de Tigné Gérard Depardieu AC Anjou 93   14
                                                        Terroirs
Owned by the French actor. 100% Cabernet Franc aged
in oak. Deep saturation with dense smoky tones. Hint of
woodland fruits and smoke shows promise. Plenty of
tannin to ensure good ageing potential.

Red between £10 and £12

**Cuvée des Variennes du Grand Clos Charles Joguet
AC Chinon 88**   13
(Searsons)   *Wine merchants/off licences*
Aromas of violets and wood shavings carry through on
flavour with a keen edge of acidity and slight herbaceous
finish. Best served cool.

ROSÉ WINES

Rosé between £4.50 and £5.25

Remy Pannier AC Rosé d'Anjou 93   13
(Barry & Fitzwilliam)   *Widely available*
Definite strawberry fruits and medium acidity

.Rosé between £5.25 and £6.50

B & G AC Rosé d'Anjou 93   12
(Dillons)   *Widely available*
Produced from the Cabernet Franc and Grolleau grapes.
Pleasant raspberry flavour ending on a dry finish.

Rosé between £6.50 and £8

★ **Château de Pimpean AC Cabernet d'Anjou 93**   15

Terroirs

Onion skinned in colour. Surprisingly good strawberry
fruit aromas with just a hint of chocolate. Fruit bursting
out with limey acidity and long fruit finish yet dry. One
of the best tasted.

La Rosétte AC Rosé d'Anjou 94   12
(Gilbeys)   *Widely available*
Perfect summer drinking. Raspberry colour, vigorous
fruit and very pleasant fruity yet dry finish.

Rosé between £10 and £12

Joquet Jeunes Vignes AC Chinon 93   13
(Brangan)   *Wine merchants/off licences*
Very pale, hints of strawberry fruits. Long lingering
finish.

Rhône

The region is long and narrow, stretching from Lyon to past Avignon. It is easier to understand when divided into two areas: the Northern Rhône and the Southern Rhône, which produce very distinctive styles of wine.

Styles of Northern Rhône

Located in a narrow valley, Northern Rhône vineyards are planted on steep terraced granite slopes—a beautiful landscape, but it is difficult to tend the vineyards. The valley is cut through by the Rhône river and vineyards flank both the right and left banks. The area produces powerful majestic red wines requiring years to mature from the Syrah grape and aromatic white wines from the Viognier grape.

Styles of Southern Rhône

Moving south from the town of Montélimar, steep terraces give way to vineyards that broaden out into vast plains. The area produces all styles of wine, from a greater variety of grapes than in the North, from everyday drinking reds to spicy full-bodied styles. Rosé, still white, sparkling and dessert wines are also produced. Highly respected shippers from the region include Jaboulet, Chapoutier, Chave, Guigal and Fleury.

Northern Rhône wines available in Ireland

Côte Rôtie: Reputed to be where the first vines were planted in France. Powerful exciting reds which require at least ten years to open up. For red wine production a small amount of Viognier is added to the blend. At their most excellent from Guigal's single vineyard are La Mouline, La Landonne and La Turque.

Condrieu: White wines produced exclusively from the Viognier grape. Very small area.

Château Grillet, with only 20 hectares, is the smallest AC wine in France for white wine.

Cornas: Red wines produced from 100% Syrah. Intense and spicy.

Hermitage: The Syrah grape from vineyards on the hill of Hermitage produces intense powerful spicy red wines, which need time to mature. Along with Côte Rôtie and Cornas, it is considered to be one of the finest red wines of the Rhône. White wine is also produced from Marsanne and Roussanne grapes.

Crozes-Hermitage: Red and white wines are produced from the same grape varieties as Hermitage. A larger area than Hermitage, quality is not so high.

St Joseph: On the western bank of the river; red and white wines are produced. Styles are more approachable than their powerful neighbours.

St Péray: Known principally for its sparkling wine production, still white wine is also produced.

Southern Rhône wines available in Ireland

Côtes du Rhône: Red, white and rosé wines. Reds are produced from Grenache, Syrah, Mourvèdre, Carignan and Terret Noir. Whites are made from Marsanne, Roussanne, Clairette and Ugni Blanc.

Côtes du Rhône-Villages: Slightly higher in alcohol content and quality, these wines come from one of seventeen specific communes. The name of the commune appears on the label. Communes include Visan, Vacqueyras and Rasteau. White and rosé are also made.

Côtes du Ventoux: Red and rosé wines are made from Grenache, Syrah, Cinsaut and Carignan, white are made from Clairette and Bourboulenc.

Gigondas: Delicious spicy deeply coloured red wines are produced here, along with a little rosé. Up to 80% Grenache is used with other varieties, including Syrah, Mourvèdre and Cinsaut.

Tavel: Famous for its spicy dry rosé wine production.

Châteauneuf-du-Pape: One of France's most famous red

wines, the AC is located around the city of Avignon. Thirteen grape varieties are permitted in the blend, including Grenache, Syrah, Mourvèdre and Cinsaut. Rich in alcohol and savoury flavour, the best of them need at least eight years to show their potential. Less traditional styles can be drunk young. The vineyards take their name from the thirteenth-century papacy of Pope Clement V at Avignon. Domaine-bottled Châteauneuf-du-Pape is distinguished by the papal coat of arms embossed on the bottle. White Châteauneuf can be a wonderful drink whose popularity is growing, even though the AC represents only a tiny percentage of overall production.

Coteaux du Tricastin: Red, rosé and white wines covering a large area. Usually good value.

Côtes du Lubéron: Just beginning to be seen on Irish shelves; red, white and rosé are produced.

Clairette de Die: Still or sparkling. Sparkling wines are produced from the Clairette and Muscat grapes.

Vins de Pays include Collines Rhodaniennes, Coteaux de l'Ardèche and VDP de la Drôme.

Vins Doux Naturels: Muscat de Beaumes-de-Venise is the most famous sweet wine from the region. Rasteau VDN is produced from Grenache. Several styles are produced, with Rancio the best known. It indicates a wine which has been matured in cask, usually in the open air, for some years.

WHITE WINES

White between £5.25 and £6.50

La Vieille Ferme AC Côtes du Lubéron 93   13
(Allied Drinks)   *Wine merchants/off licences*
Up-and-coming appellation from the southern Rhône. Good fruit appeal with a medium long finish.

Whites between £6.50 and £8

Château Val Joanis AC Côtes du Lubéron 93   13
(Gilbeys)   *Wine merchants/off licences*

Paul Jaboulet Aîné Parallèle 45 AC Côtes du Rhône 92
(Gilbeys)   *Widely available*   12
Hints of purple. Good layers of soft fruits and medium
to long finish.

Vidal Fleury AC Côtes du Rhône 91   14
(Fitzgeralds)   *Wine merchants/off licences*
Firm structure with chewy fruit and supple tannins
make this a good example of basic Côtes du Rhône.

Visan AC Côtes du Rhône-Villages 91   12
(Syrah Wines)   *Widely available*
Attractive presentation. Raspberry colour delivers on
fruits with that pleasant hint of spice associated with the
Rhône. Easy drinking.

Reds between £8 and £10

Caves St Pierre AC Gigondas 92   14
(Febvre)   *Widely available*
Rhône red wines are muscular in style. This spicy Syrah
with its magnificent depth of colour and pungent fruit
aromas in an earthy style is an excellent example.

**Cuvée de la Reine Jeanne Ogier AC Châteauneuf-du-Pape
89**   12
(Remy)   *Widely available*
Pleasant forward fruit tones with good spice and a hint
of liquorice. Good structure with nice length to the
finish.

Domaine du Vieux Chêne AC Côtes du Rhône-Villages 92
(Brangan)   *Wine merchants/off licences*   14
Well balanced. Spice and stewed red berry fruit fla-
vours.

**Domaine le Vieux Micocoulier AC Coteaux du Tricastin
90**   13
(Moore)   *Wine merchants/off licences*
Meaty and chunky. Powerful stuff.

Jean-Louis Grippat AC St Joseph 89   13
(Searsons)   *Wine merchants/off licences*
Vibrant fruit. Smooth texture. Held together with
harmonious yet robust tannins.

Labouré-Roi AC Châteauneuf-du-Pape 93   12
                                    Quinnsworth
Easy-drinking example of this AC. Don't expect too
much concentration but enjoy the soft red berry fruit
tones and spicy finish.

Paul Jaboulet Aîné Pierre Aiguille AC Gigondas 90 14
(Gilbeys)   *Wine merchants/off licences*
Big in style. Deep purple tones. Lots of spicy sweet fruit
attack and a bite of spice on the finish.

Paul Jaboulet Aîné Les Jalets AC Crozes-Hermitage 92
(Gilbeys)   *Wine merchants/off licences*   14
Rich concentrated fruit with a silky texture overlain with
a meaty extract.

Romane-Machotte Pierre Amadieu AC Gigondas 90 14
(Syrah Wines)   *Wine merchants/off licences*
Chunky and packed with damson and plummy fruits.
Firm structure with a good strong finish. Good value/
quality.

Reds between £10 and £12

★ **Alain Graillot AC Crozes-Hermitage 93**   15
(Syrah Wines)   *Wine merchants/off licences*
Highly commended. Good choice for a 93 red Rhône.
Deep and concentrated with an earthy tone and powerful
spicy and meaty finish.

★★ **La Bernardine Chapoutier AC Châteauneuf-du-Pape 92**
(Grants)   *Wine merchants/off licences*   16
Produced from 40–60-year-old vines, this is a real
stunner. Cold tea aromas with excellent fruit and tannin
balance. The wine opens, develops and lingers. Mind the
high alcohol!

Mazurd et Fils Grand Réserve AC Côtes du Rhône 85
(Syrah Wines)   *Wine merchants/off licences*   13
Already showing age at the rim. All the hallmarks of
mature mellow strawberry fruits overlain with the
pepper of Syrah. Has reached its plateau of maturity.

★ **Notre Dame des Cellettes Domaine Ste Anne AC Côtes
du Rhône-Villages 92**   15
(Brangan)   *Wine merchants/off licences*
Packs a punch in an earthy plummy young Syrah style.
Fruit, tannin and acidity all combine to give a long
finish.

Paul Jaboulet Aîné Le Grand Pompée AC St Joseph 94
(Gilbeys)   *Wine merchants/off licences*   13
Silky textured but with concentrated fruit and tannin
giving opulence and style.

★ **Paul Jaboulet Aîné Les Cèdres AC Châteauneuf-du Pape 93**
(Gilbeys)   *Wine merchants/off licences*   15
Lots of strong meaty/peppery tones with good bitter-
sweet cherry fruits that attack and fan out on the palate.
Better on the palate than the nose. Ends on a high note
with tannins taking over from the fruit.

Reds between £12 and £15

★ **Domaine Chante Perdrix AC Châteauneuf-du-Pape 89**
(Moore)   *Wine merchants/off licences*   15
Mature wine with tobacco scents. Good mix of depth of
fruit and maturity.

Domaine de la Mordorée AC Châteauneuf-du-Pape 91
(Brangan)   *Wine merchants/off licences*   14
This elegant wine has a rich colour, superb fruit and a
long intense satisfying finish.

Reds between £15 and £20

★ **Clos des Papes AC Châteauneuf-du-Pape 92**   15
(Syrah Wines)   *Wine merchants/off licences*
Big, bold and still young. Good attack of fruit and long,
long finish.

★ **Domaine de Monterpuis AC Châteauneuf-du-Pape 92**
(Syrah Wines)   *Wine merchants/off licences*   15
Good deep concentrated fruit with plenty of balancing
acidity and lots of drying tannins indicating youth.
Watch how it will develop. Super wine.

★ **Domaine Lucien Barrot et Fils AC Châteauneuf-du-
Pape 93**   15
(Callaghan)   *Wine merchants/off licences*
Brick in colour. Complex aromas of strawberry with
hints of tobacco, and a rich concentrated finish.

★ **Domaine Ste Anne Syrah AC Côtes du Rhône 90**   15
(Brangan)   *Wine merchants/off licences*
Meaty, saucy aromas which develop and linger long
after swallowing. Tannins are supple. Overall texture is
like velvet.

★ **Paul Jaboulet Ainé La Chapelle AC Hermitage 89**   15
(Gilbeys)   *Wine merchants/off licences*
Deep garnet with purple tones. Complex aromas from
spicy Syrah fruit to mature tobacco and liquorice. As the
wine matures animal scents become apparent. Finishes
on a long opulent note.

Reds between £20 and £30

★★ **Domaine Vieux Télégraphe AC Châteauneuf-du-Pape
92**   16
(Findlaters)   *Wine merchants/off licences*
Big and powerful. Full of savoury meaty extract cut
through with fine fruits needing time to evolve. It packs
a punch.

★ Guigal AC Hermitage 90
(Syrah Wines)   *Wine merchants/off licences*   16
Benchmark classic style full of meaty extract. Fruit still
tight-knit and closed. Needs more time to express itself.
Notice the sheer depth of colour, the wonderful spice of
Syrah and the extraordinary length on the finish.

South

The South of France covers the areas of Languedoc, Roussillon and Provence. Modern vinification methods combined with local innovation and flying Australian winemakers are strongly influencing the styles of wine now produced. Fruitier, well-structured wines are becoming widely available, offering great value for money.

Languedoc

The region produces the greatest amount of Vin de Table in France, and over 80 per cent of its Vin de Pays. It is also famed for its Vins Doux Naturels (dessert wines).

Roussillon

Often considered more Catalan than French, there is a strong Spanish influence here.

Both areas cover the departments of the Aude, Hérault, Gard and Pyrénées-Orientals.

Provence

Vines have been planted here since 600 BC. Every type of wine is made—red, white, rosé and sparkling. World famous for its rosés, there are extremely exciting red wines being produced. A confusing area, stretching as it does from Nice to Marseilles, 80% of the wines produced are drunk in France. There is a big export drive under way, and world-wide exports have more than doubled since 1980.

Styles of Languedoc-Roussillon

From simply easy drinking Vin de Table, to Vin de Pays, to AC. All styles are produced—white, red, rosé, sparkling and dessert.

Languedoc-Roussillon wines available in Ireland

Coteaux du Languedoc: A very large and varied AC area covering red and white wine production. Within this vast zone are smaller sub-regions of higher-quality AC wines such as Faugères and St Chinian.

Côtes de Roussillon: Soft silky red wines with AC Collioure producing powerful full-bodied reds.

Côtes du Roussillon-Villages: This AC covers only red wines.

Fitou: For red wines only. The best should be big and spicy.

Minervois: Red wine production dominates, but high-standard white and rosé wines are also produced. The trick is to find your own particular favourite.

Corbières: Mostly red wines, with white and rosé also being produced. White wines can be very good. Amongst the many *Vins de Pays* from the region the ones available in Ireland include VDP de l'Hérault, VDP du Gard, VDP de Montcaume, VDP d'Oc, VDP Catalan, VDP Pyrénées-Orientales, VDP Cassan, VDP de l'Aude.

Vin Doux Naturel: This is naturally sweet fortified wine. The whites are produced from the Muscat grape. Reds are produced from the Grenache. *Muscat de Rivesaltes*, *Muscat de Frontignan* and *Banyuls* are available in Ireland.

Styles of Provence

White, red and rosé are produced. Rosés are often pale and onion-skinned in colour. White wines need to be drunk young as they lose freshness quickly. Reds have a remarkable cerise colour with lots of herby and spicy aromas and flavours.

Provence wines available in Ireland

Bandol, which produces white, red and rosé wines. By law red wines are produced from a minimum of 50% Mourvèdre and must spend 18 months in cask before bottling. They have great ageing ability.

Coteaux d'Aix-en-Provence: AC status was awarded in 1985. Main production is red with white and rosé also being produced. Red wines are very fruity and at their best served cool.

Côtes de Provence: 60% of production is devoted to rosé wine, with red and white also being produced. Rosés are famous for their fruity yet dry styles. Other appellations include *Bellet*, *Palette* and *Cassis*, three tiny areas rarely seen outside their region.

Coteaux de Pierrevert: This area is one of the highest vineyards in France and produces red, white and rosé wines under the VDQS category.

Coteaux Varois: Another VDQS category created in 1985, producing red, white and rosé.

WHITE WINES

Whites under £4.50

La Carignano Chardonnay VDP Cassan 94   13
Dunnes Stores

Apple fruit aromas and flavours cut through by balanced lively acidity to give a crisp finish.

Vin du Patron Chardonnay VDP d'Oc 94   12
Quinnsworth

Attack of fruit on the palate is strong, if a bit awkward. The oak influence imparts structure.

Whites between £4.50 and £5.25

Calvet Chardonnay VDP d'Oc 94   12
(Grants)   *Wine merchants/off licences*

Hints of peachy aromas with quite a weighty mouth-feel. Good balance between fruit and acidity and a medium long finish.

Domaine de la Tuilerie (Hugh Ryman) Chardonnay VDP d'Oc 94   13
Quinnsworth

Fat and weighty with good fruit development and nice length to finish.

Fortant de France Sauvignon Blanc VDP d'Oc 94   12
(Fitzgeralds)   *Widely available*
Produced from 100% Sauvignon Blanc, the wine is full
of citrus fruit flavours—ruby grapefruit springs to mind.

★ **Laperouse VDP d'Oc 94**   16
                                               Quinnsworth
Peach type fruits with fresh acidity. Penfolds and Val
d'Orbieu have combined to express all the best in winemaking techniques—a star is born!

Les Heritages Chardonnay VDP Cassan 94   14
                                             Dunnes Stores
Creamy vanilla oak with hints of exotic fruits and a
toasty pleasant finish.

Les Meuliers AC Minervois 94   13
(MacCormaic)   *Widely available*
Hint of vanilla confirms the oak influence. Nice harmoni-
ous balance with good fruit and length in finish.

Pezilla AC Côtes du Roussillon nv   12
(Barry & Fitzwilliam)   *Wine merchants/off licences*
Ripe fruit flavours of pears and peach.

Prestige Des Calaberts VDP Coteaux de l'Ardèche 93 12
(Ecock)   *Widely available*
Nice example of the good value wines coming from the
South of France. Don't expect complexity—just enjoy the
freshness.

Val d'Orbieu Mediterre VDP d'Oc nv   13
                                               Findlaters
Ripe fruits fan out on the palate and give length to the
finish.

Whites between £5.25 and £6.50

Camplon Peyres Nobles AC Corbières 94   12
(MacCormaic)   *Widely available*
Nice mineral tone to the aroma of this wine. Well

DUNNES STORES

*Enjoy the exciting new additions to our already
extensive wine range - many bought directly
from the vineyards*

From the South of France - *La Carignano*, easy-drinking
Chardonnays, Merlots, Syrahs, Cabernet Sauvignons at
reasonable prices. *Chateaux Flaugergues*, a recent winner
of the coveted Golden Grape Award from *La Guide
Hachette*. *Chateau de Gourgazuad*, highly acclaimed by
international wine writers.

From Burgundy - Fine red and white wines from *Maison
Pierre Ponnelle* whose winemaker, Bernard Repolt, is
internationally respected.

From Italy- Quality examples of Chianti and Vino Nobile
di Montepulciano are from the *Badia Alle Corti* Estate in
the heart of Tuscany.

From Portugal - *Tinto da Talha* is a fine example of the
exciting styles emerging from this dynamic wine country.

From Australia - Our *Moyston* and *Seppelt Labels* come
exclusively from the Penfold Winery.

From Chile - Try our red and white wines from the *San
Pedro Winery* which is under the guidance of Jacques
Lurton of the renowned winemaking family of Bordeaux.

BETTER QUALITY AND VALUE

THE BRAND OF QUALITY

balanced with fruit showing through on the end.

Château Maris AC Minervois 93   13
(MacCormaic)   *Widely available*
Produced from 100% Maccabeu. Good aromatic tones
with balanced lively acidity and a clean finish.

Domaine de Bosc VDP Hérault 94   14
(Cassidy)   *Widely available*
Has a super 'nettle' nose—the hallmark of good
Sauvignon Blanc. Delivers on taste and ends with a zip
on the finish.

Domaine des Anges AC Côtes du Ventoux 94   12
(Karwig)   *Wine merchants/off licences*
The white Rhône varieties Marsanne and Rousanne add
peachy fruit while the Bourboulenc gives a touch of
acidity.

Fortant de France Chardonnay VDP d'Oc 94   13
(Fitzgeralds)   *Widely available*
Oak-influenced Chardonnay characteristics with melon-
type aromas and flavours and just a hint of vanilla.
Good length on the finish.

Philippe de Baudin Chardonnay VDP d'Oc 93   14
                                                    Quinnsworth
Very much in the Oz style. Exotic fruit tones and
appealing oak influence.

Philippe de Baudin Sauvignon Blanc VDP d'Oc 94   13
                                                    Quinnsworth
Herbaceous grassy tones with quite a long finish.

Piat Chardonnay VDP d'Oc 93   13
(Gilbeys)   *Widely available*
Delivers on fruit with good balance of acidity and
alcohol. Warm ripe fruit style.

Whites between £6.50 and £8

Blanc de Brau VDP Côtes de Lastours 94   13
(Brangan)   *Wine merchants/off licences*
Apple blossom aromas with good clean fruit attack
ending in a spicy overtone.

Château des Lanes Grenache en Vert AC Corbières 93   13
(Karwig)   *Wine merchants/off licences*
From the Montagne d'Alaric. Extra lively acidity, with
enough fruit to give some balance.

Cuvée Octagon Viognier VDP 94   13
(Searsons)   *Wine merchants/off licences*
The fashionable white grape of the 90s. This has lots of
ripe peachy fruit with just a hint of residual sugar to
make it the perfect apéritif wine.

Domaine de Brau Chardonnay VDP 93   12
(Brangan)   *Wine merchants/off licences*
Lightly oaked. Vanilla tones with ripe kiwi-like fruits
and a hint of toast on the finish.

Domaine de Coussergues Chardonnay VDP d'Oc 94 13
(Febvre)   *Wine merchants/off licences*
Refined wine with underlying flavours of tropical fruits
balanced by good acidity.

James Herrick Chardonnay VDP d'Oc 94   14
                    Wines Direct
Melon-type fruits with balancing acidity and clean fresh
finish.

Whites between £8 and £10

**Domaine de l'Arjolle Muscat Petits Grains VDP Côtes
de Thongue 94**   13
(Brangan)   *Wine merchants/off licences*
Intensely flavoured with low acidity marked with a
delicious grapey finish. Try it with fine pâtés.

Domaine de Terre Megere VDP d'Oc 94   13
(Brangan)   *Wine merchants/off licences*
Produced from the Viognier grape. Peaches and cream
come through and linger briefly.

Domaine des Anges Chardonnay VDP Vaucluse 94 14
(Karwig)   *Wine merchants/off licences*
Golden in colour with subtle creamy Chardonnay tones.
Very clean and fresh on the palate with lots of balance
and enough fruit to carry through to the long finish.

  White between £10 and £12

Rolle Vermentino VDP Var 94   13
(Brangan)   *Wine merchants/off licences*
A balanced wine with good acidity and lovely aromas of
exotic fruits. A delicate yet elegant finish.

RED WINES

  Reds under £4.50

La Carignano Cabernet Sauvignon VDP Cassan 94 12
Dunnes Stores
Purple-toned with stalky red berry fruit aromas. Nicely
balanced. Good length on the finish. A good food wine.

La Carignano Merlot VDP Cassan 94   13
Dunnes Stores
Soft easy-drinking. Good jammy-type cassis fruits and
some length on finish.

La Carignano Syrah VDP Cassan 94   14
Dunnes Stores
Savoury spicy nose with good garnet colours. Flavour-
some attack of ripe fruits finishing in a bite of pepper.

  Red between £4.50 and £5.25

Alexis Lichine Merlot VDP d'Oc 93   13
(Greenhills)   *Wine merchants/off licences*
Appealing garnet colour. Good flavour in an easy-
drinking style.

Blue Nun VDP Gard nv   13
(Dillons)   *Widely available*

All the ripe red berry fruits of a hot climate. Easy
appeal.

Calvet Cabernet Sauvignon VDP d'Oc 94   13
(Grants)   *Wine merchants/off licences*

Medium-bodied with forward ripe-berry fruits in an
easy to drink approachable style.

Calvet Syrah VDP d'Oc 94   14
(Grants)   *Wine merchants/off licences*

Young Syrah with a typical deep crimson/purple
colour, spicy jammy fruit ending in a high note of
flavour. Good value.

**Cuvée Antoine de Montpezad AC Coteaux du
Languedoc 94**   14
                                            Dunnes Stores

Produced from 100% Syrah. Well structured with hints
of tobacco. Ripe berry fruits follow through on flavour.
Good choice with food.

Domaine de Rivoyre Cabernet Sauvignon VDP d'Oc 93 13
                                              Quinnsworth

Blackcurrant fruit with decent structure and a good bite
of tannin and acidity.

★**Domaine Ste Nathalie AC Faugères 94**   15
                                            Dunnes Stores

Damson and plum fruits with a silky texture, supple
tannins and balanced acidity. A luscious drink with
good length on the finish.

Fortant de France Cabernet Sauvignon VDP d'Oc 93 14
(Fitzgeralds)   *Widely available*
Shows what Cabernet Sauvignon in a warm climate
produced by modern methods can achieve. Clean
blackcurrant aromas. Good structure and a supple finish

overlain with oak influence.

Fortant de France Merlot VDP d'Oc 93   13
(Fitzgeralds)   *Widely available*
Lots of plummy fruits overlain with a hint of spice in a
smooth silky finish.

Gamay VDP Coteaux de l'Ardèche 93   12
(Ecock)   *Wine merchants/off licences*
Raspberry fruit tones, packed up with fresh acidity.
Enjoy now.

Pezilla AC Côtes du Roussillon 93   13
(Barry & Fitzwilliam)   *Wine merchants/off licences*
Great party wine—easy to drink with a slight pleasant
bitterness to the finish.

Val d'Orbieu Mediterre VDP d'Oc nv   14
(Findlaters)   *Wine merchants/off licences*
Intense in colour and aroma, full of tempting bittersweet
fruit ending in a long finish.

Reds between £5.25 and £6.50

B & G Cabernet Sauvignon VDP d'Oc 93   13
(Dillons)   *Widely available*
Good fruit, good acidity and good balance, with a long
finish.

B & G Merlot VDP d'Oc 93   13
(Dillons)   *Wine merchants/off licences*
Dark ruby in colour with intense cedar aromas.

Camplon Peyres Nobles AC Corbierès 93   12
(MacCormaic)   *Wine merchants/off licences*
Deep garnet colour with lots of creamy oak influence
and creamy fruits. Low to medium acidity, drinking
well now.

★ **Château Cazal Viel AC St Chinian 92** 15

Quinnsworth

Appetising with rich meaty extract. Fruit backed up
with harmonious tannins and bite. Good value/quality
ratio. Very good food wine.

Château de Brau AC Cabardes 94 14

(Brangan) *Wine merchants/off licences*

Deep purple in colour with mouth-watering rich fruit
tones that fan out and linger on the finish.

Château de Combelle AC St Chinian 90 12

(Gilbeys) *Wine merchants/off licences*

Purple-tinged, with brambly fruit and medium length.

Château La Grave AC Minervois 93 14

(Searsons) *Wine merchants/off licences*

Four-square Minervois with its herb-like aromas,
bracing acidity, good alcohol and balanced length.

Château Milhau-Lacugue AC St Chinian 92 13

Quinnsworth

Big cherry wine—full on the palate with a long finish.
Good food wine.

★**Domaine Coste Rouge AC Coteaux du Languedoc 93** 15

Dunnes Stores

A very appealing spicy Syrah, overlain with vanilla
tones. Good attack of fruit finishing with just a hint of
chocolate. Balanced acidity.

Domaine de Thelin Merlot VDP d'Oc 92 13

(Karwig) *Wine merchants/off licences*

Fruit-cake aromas and flavours with a supple texture.

Domaine des Pourthié VDP Hérault 90 13

(Cassidy) *Wine merchants/off licences*

Herby tones with a mouthful of fruit backed up with
supple tannins. Smooth on the finish. Enjoy now.

[156]

Domaine Maris Carte Noir AC Minervois 90   14
(MacCormaic)   *Wine merchants/off licences*
Squashed ripe berry fruit tones with good concentration
and an attractive peppery bite on the finish.

Domaine St Germain AC Minervois 92   14
(MacCormaic)   *Wine merchants/off licences*
Produced from a blend of Syrah, Grenache and
Carignan. Good structure, supple tannins overlain with
vanilla.

Figaro VDP Hérault 93   14
(Allied Drinks)   *Wine merchants/off licences*
Cerise in colour. Meaty nose with soft tannins and
medium length to finish.

★**Laperouse VDP d'Oc 94**   15
                                              Quinnsworth
An exciting wine, with restrained fruit. Full of structure
and balance with lingering fruit flavours.

Le Piat de Merlot VDP d'Oc 93   13
(Gilbeys)   *Widely available*
Herb, thyme and rosemary come to mind. Soft supple
tannins. Good with food.

Les Terrasses de Guilhem VDP Hérault 92   14
(Allied Drinks)   *Wine merchants/off licences*
Deep purple in colour. Big and meaty, typical of the old
traditional style.

Philippe de Baudin Cabernet Sauvignon VDP d'Oc 93   14
                                              Quinnsworth
Lots of blackberry fruit influence with hints of vanilla
and soft supple tannins.

Philippe de Baudin Merlot VDP d'Oc 92   14
                                              Quinnsworth
All the velvet texture and suppleness of Merlot with
lingering red berry fruit flavours.

Piat Cabernet Sauvignon VDP d'Oc 93   12
(Gilbeys)   *Widely available*
Good attack of ripe fruits on the palate which fan out
and end in an uncomplicated pleasant easy-drinking
style.

Reds between £6.50 and £8

Château de Blomac AC Minervois 91   13
(Karwig)   *Wine merchants/off licences*
A soft and approachable style with dried fruit tones and
good length.

★ **Château de Gourgazaud Réserve AC Minervois 92**   15
Dunnes Stores
Concentrated aromas and flavours of wild red berry
fruits and herbs. A trace of vanilla combines with
integrated tannins to end in a long supple finish.

Château St Auriol AC Corbières 92   14
(Searsons)   *Wine merchants/off licences*
A big chewy wine. Lots of dense red berry fruits
overlain with a slight meatiness.

Cuvée de l'Arjolle VDP Côtes de Thongues 93   13
(Brangan)   *Wine merchants/off licences*
Produced from 70% Cabernet Sauvignon and 30%
Merlot. Rich in both fruit and aroma. Big spicy finish.

★ **Domaine Clavel 'La Méjanelle' AC Coteaux de
Languedoc 93**   *Wines Direct*   15
Deep cerise in colour. Packed with delicious blackcurrant
and herb-like flavours. An extremely interesting wine,
with a long pleasant finish.

★ **Domaine de la Baume VDP d'Oc 92**   15
Quinnsworth
Terrific red wine drinking. Packs a punch with fruit and
acidity. Finishes with lots of vanilla overtones.

Domaine de Limbardie VDP Coteaux de Murviel 93 14
(Brangan) *Wine merchants/off licences*
Intense concentration—just observe the colour—
appetising meaty aroma and excellent structure.

**Domaine de Terre Megere Les Dolomies AC Coteaux
de Languedoc 94** 14
(Brangan) *Wine merchants/off licences*
Fruit flavours with supple tannins and ripe juicy fruit
make for delicious easy-drinking.

Domaine du Grand Crès AC Corbières 92 14
Wines Direct
Deep purple in colour with attractive ripe flavours of
plum and fig. Nice lingering finish with lots of spicy
tones.

Domaine Ste Eulalie AC Minervois 94 13
(Karwig) *Wine merchants/off licences*
Big herb-like aromas with plenty of character and good
balance between tannins and acidity.

Reds between £8 and £10

Château de Lastours AC Corbières 91 14
(Brangan) *Wine merchants/off licences*
A 'bold' wine in terms of both aroma and flavour. Big
port-like finish.

★★ **Château Flaugergues La Méjanelle AC Coteaux du
Languedoc 93** 16
Dunnes Stores
Matured in oak, a delicious big ripe powerful wine full
of raspberry mousse flavours and concentrated rich
tannins. Impressive long finish.

**Domaine de la Vallongue AC Coteaux d'Aix en
Provence Les Baux 91** 13
(MacCormaic) *Wine merchants/off licences*
Big on fruit with ripe tannins, good depth of flavour and
a spicy finish.

★ **Domaine des Anges Clos de la Tour AC Côtes du Ventoux 90** 15
(Karwig) *Wine merchants/off licences*
Very deep saturation of colour. Aromas of plum and even fig float on the air. A big-bodied, satisfying wine with lots of structure. Mouth-drying tannin ensures a long life.

Domaine du Vieux Chêne VDP Vaucluse 94 13
(Brangan) *Wine merchants/off licences*
Still very young. Bags of fruit with very forward tannins and quite high acidity. A big mouthful of red berry fruits.

Reds between £10 and £12

Château de Lastours AC Corbières 90 14
(Brangan) *Wine merchants/off licences*
Raisiny fruit with hints of figs and leather make for a rich full-bodied style.

Château Haut Gléon AC Corbières 91 14
(Jenkinson) *Wine merchants/off licences*
Rich and spicy with good structure and concentrated red berry fruit flavours.

Domaine Bunan Mas de la Rouvière AC Bandol 89 14
(Mackenway) *Wine merchants/off licences*
A blend of 65% Mourvèdre, 14% Grenache, 6% Syrah and 15% Cinsaut aged for 18 months in oak barriques all add up to a wine of powerful herb-like aromas and flavours with a rich spicy finish.

Reds between £12 and £15

★ **Domaine Tempier AC Bandol 90** 15
(Brangan) *Wine merchants/off licences*
A top example of Bandol. Produced from the Mourvèdre grape and aged in oak, this is a powerful example of the plummy and cedary tones the grape imparts.

★**Mas de Daumas Gassac VDP Hérault 93**   16
(Allied Drinks)   *Wine merchants/off licences*
Produced principally from Cabernet Sauvignon,
Cabernet Franc, Merlot, Syrah and Malbec the wine has
immense structure with assertive fruit and herb flavours
overladen with a smoky mineral touch. Needs at least
five years to show its quality.

Red between £15 and £20

★**Domaine de Trevallon Les Baux AC Bandol 92**   15
(Brangan)   *Wine merchants/off licences*
Like walking through a field of wild herbs with smokey
bacon wafting through the air! This wine demands
attention and concentration due to its complexity. Still
young, something very good and different.

ROSÉ WINES

Rosé between £4.50 and £5.25

Fortant de France Rosé Syrah VDP d'Oc 94   13
(Fitzgeralds)   *Wine merchants/off licences*
Produced from 100% Syrah. Intense cherry aromas and
flavours finishing in a dry style.

Rosés between £5.25 and £6.50

Château de Flaugergues AC Coteaux du Languedoc 93   13
                              Dunnes Stores
Fresh and clean tasting with hints of strawberry fruits in
an off-dry style.

Domaine de Brau VDQS Cabardès 94   11
(Brangan)   *Wine merchants/off licences*
Salmon tinged in colour with quite an earthy aroma. For
drinking young.

Les Calanques AC Côtes de Provence 92   13
(Febvre)   *Wine merchants/off licences*
The good development of fruit on the palate makes up
for the shortness of fruit on the nose. Surprisingly long

[162   ]

finish.

Rosé between £10 and £12

**Source de Vignelaure AC Coteaux d'Aix en Provence
94**   13
(Febvre/Parsons)   *Wine merchants/off licences*
Onion skinned rosé with hints of raspberry and good
bite of acidity.

South-West

Situated between Bordeaux and Languedoc-Roussillon, the South-West of France is a region that deserves to be better known.

A vast range of red, white, rosé, sparkling and dessert wines is produced. The spirit Armagnac also hails from this part of France. There is a wide range of Appellation Contrôlée and Vin de Pays wines. Reds are noted for their rich dark colour, are big on flavour, and can taste of new oak. Whites are fresh and appealing in a crisp zesty style. Rosé wines are usually dry yet fruity. Dessert wines are rich and honeyed. Sparkling wines are top quality.

Bergerac: Red wines are produced from the classic Bordeaux mix of grapes, with Merlot often dominating. Widely available in Ireland. Whites should be fresh with greengage fruit flavours. Rosé wines are usually strawberry-tinted with good fruit and a dry finish. The reds are deeply coloured with ripe red berry fruit appeal.

Pécharmant: Considered one of the best red wines of the region.

Côtes de Duras: Red and white wines.

Gaillac: More white is produced than red, along with a style known as *perlé* (faintly bubbly).

Montravel: Dry to sweet.

Monbazillac: Produces the most famous sweet wine of the region.

Buzet: Red wine.

Irouléguy: Red, white and rosé wines.

Côtes du Frontonnais: The local grape Négrette is used in the blend for this red wine.

Côtes du Marmandais: Red is made from a variety of grapes; some white and rosé also produced.

Cahors: A famous red wine from one of the oldest vineyards in France; traditionally known as the 'black wine of Cahors' due to its dark colour. Dominant grape variety is the Malbec (known locally as Auxerrois). This wine is not as available as it should be. It has two styles—the traditional is a big delicious mouthful of plummy fruits with hints of spice, while the modern style is lighter in an easy-drinking style.

Madiran: The local grape variety Tannat is used extensively in blended red wines. Madiran rivals Cahors as one of the deepest-coloured and longest-lived wines of the South of France. Unfortunately, it is not easily available.

Vin de Pays Charentais: Bone-dry wines are produced.

WHITE WINES

Whites under £5.25

Alexis Lichine VDP Côtes de Gascogne nv　　　　12
(Greenhills)　　　　　　　　　　　　　*Widely available*
Easy-drinking. Short on fruit but has good refreshing acidity.

Domaine du Rey VDP Côtes de Gascogne 94　　　13
　　　　　　　　　　　　　　　　　　Searsons
Delivers on fresh crisp fruit and zingy acidity.

Whites between £5.25 and £6.50

Château Singleyrac AC Bergerac 94　　　　　14
(Ecock)　　　　　　　　　　　　　*Widely available*
Bottling off the lees adds texture and creaminess to white wines. This delivers on fruit and body.

Domaine de Joy VDP Côtes de Gascogne 94　　　14
(Moore)　　　　　　　　　*Wine merchants/off licences*
Fresh and crisp. Lots of lovely acidity and fresh clean finish.

Domaine du Tariquet VDP Côtes de Gascogne 94　12
(Brangan)　　　　　　　　*Wine merchants/off licences*
To be drunk young while the crisp apple fruits and lively acidity are at their freshest.

Whites between £6.50 and £8

★ **Château Jolys AC Jurançon Sec 93**   15
Wines Direct
Wonderful honeysuckle aromas with lots of fruit on the palate. Smooth with good body and fresh acidity.

Château de la Jaubertie Henry Ryman AC Bergerac 91
Mitchells   13
Quite a tight fisted style with fruit and tannins fighting for first place. Good food wine.

Grain Sauvage Blanc de Blancs AC Jurançon Sec 94 13
(Searson)   *Wine merchants/off licences*
Peachy fruit and dry yet flavoursome finish.

White between £10 and £12

Domaine Cauhapé AC Jurançon Sec 94   13
(Brangan)   *Wine merchants/off licences*
Nice tangy aromas with hints of peach. Quite full and weighty on the palate with some length to finish.

RED WINES

Reds between £10 and £12

★ **Château du Cayrou AC Cahors 89**   15
(Brangan)   *Wine merchants/off licences*
Hints of orange skin aromas, quickly overtaken by aniseed. Very tannic with fruit fighting all the way through to the long opulent finish. Excellent food wine.

Domaine de Mignaberry AC Irouléguy 90   14
(Brangan)   *Wine merchants/off licences*
Liquorice aromas with a rich ripe game overtone. A classic structure, different and exciting for the seasoned wine drinker. Still young.

Germany

Browse through the German section of many wine outlets and restaurant lists and all you see is Liebfraumilch, Niersteiner Gutes Domtal and the like. These cheap and cheerful styles have prevented the better German wines from gaining recognition. The problem is Germany's, where since the 1970s large commercial bottlers and co-operatives have flooded the growing export market with high-tech wines, devoid of character, made from very high-yielding grapes grown on unsuitable sites.

What Germany should have done is market from the top, as France does. In Germany's marginal vine-growing climate the grapes ripen slowly, enabling them to absorb more minerals from the soil, hold their acidity and produce low sugar levels, giving light, fresh and elegant wines. Its classic Riesling grape produces wines unrivalled anywhere in the world. Styles range from fruity early drinking wines to rich, honeyed dessert wines that have the ability to age for decades.

Very few top estate wines are available in Ireland, but a number of quality-conscious wine merchants are importing very good wines that deserve to be better known. The Deinhard Heritage range is a selection from five different villages. The Riesling Spätlese Serriger Schloss Saarfelser Schlossberg from the Mosel-Saar-Ruwer region is excellent, as is the Rheingau Riesling Kabinett Rauenthaler Rothenberg. Two notable red wines from the Pfalz region are the Spätburgunder (Pinot Noir) from the renowned winemaker Rainer Lingenfelder, and the Dornfelder Dirmsteiner Schwarzerde, aged in French oak for ten months.

Labelling is now simpler, bottle shapes are changing and styles are becoming drier. Whether the latter is a good thing or not is debatable. German wine is all about balance between sweetness, acidity and alcohol.

With a succession of excellent vintages since 1988, let's hope more importers take the lead and help us to trade up to the interesting wines Germany has to offer.

Main regions

Mosel-Saar-Ruwer: Along the Mosel river valley and its tributaries, the Saar and the Ruwer, in south-west Germany. Slate soil, with very steep terraced vineyards.

Rheingau: Between Hochheim and Lorch, on the river Rhine, facing due south.

Nahe: Nahe valley, between Mosel and Rheingau. Sandstone and sandy soil.

Rheinhessen: Largest region, across the Rhine from Rheingau—rolling terrain generally. Best sites at Nierstein and Oppenheim.

Pfalz: South of Rheinhessen. Warmer climate, with level and gently sloping sites. Soil—limestone and sandstone.

Baden: Southernmost area, from Heidelberg to Lake Constance—long and narrow with volcanic soil in parts.

Grape varieties

White: Riesling, Silvaner, Müller-Thurgau, Kerner. *Red:* Spätburgunder, Portugieser, Trollinger, Dornfelder.

Styles

White: 88 per cent. Ranges from dry, medium dry to sweet dessert styles. A typical young Mosel-Saar-Ruwer Riesling Kabinett style is light, fragrant with balanced apple/peach fruitiness and crisp lemony acidity.

Red: Light in colour, velvety and fiery, particularly good from Pfalz and Baden.

Rosé: Pale pink, from red grapes, closer in style to white wine than red.

Sparkling: Deutscher Sekt—made by the tank method—less austere and less alcohol than French sparkling wine.

Producers

Co-operatives, large estates/merchants, small private growers.

Quality status

Quality is classified by the ripeness of the grapes at harvest.

Deutscher Tafelwein (DTW): Table wine.

Deutscher Tafelwein Landwein (LTW): Table wine.

Qualitätswein bestimmter Anbaugebiete (QbA): Quality wine.

Qualitätswein mit Prädikat (QmP) (six grades): Kabinett—fully ripened grapes; Spätlese—late picked; Auslese—selected pickings; Beerenauslese—noble rot, very high natural sugar; Trockenbeerenauslese—noble rot, very high natural sugar; Eiswein—picked while frozen.

Labels

AP Nr.: Quality control number on quality wines.

Abfüllung: Bottling.

DLG: National gold, silver and bronze awards.

Erzeugerabfüllung: Made and bottled by producer.

Halbtrocken: Medium dry.

Trocken: Dry.

Hochgewächs: Top estate 100% Riesling.

Weingut: Wine estate.

Weissherbst: Rosé from a single grape variety.

Winzergenossenschaft: Co-operative cellar.

Catherine Griffith

WHITE WINES

Whites under £4.50

Goldener Oktober Liebfraumilch QbA 94   12
(Grants)   *Widely available*
Light and fruity with crisp acidity in an off-dry style. Drink chilled and fresh.

Schmitt Sohne Liebfraumilch Rheinhessen QbA 94   12
Dunnes Stores
Crisp acidity gives overall balance to the ripe apple skin flavours. Nice easy drinking.

Whites between £4.50 and £5.25

Blue Nun Liebfraumilch QbA 93   11
(Dillons)   *Widely available*
Universal appeal for the novice wine drinker with its off-dry finish.

Carl Windsor Bereich Bernkastel QbA 94   13
(Greenhills)   *Widely available*
Off-dry style. Good fruit and acidity balance.

Goldener Oktober Riesling QbA 93   13
(Grants)   *Widely available*
Plenty of Riesling fruit with a characteristic slight hint of apples. Good flavour ending in a pleasant fruity finish. Drink young and fresh.

Rheinhessen Spätlese Niersteiner QmP 92   13
(Greenhills)   *Widely available*
Crisp acidity, off-dry finish and lingering length. For the drinker who likes some sweetness.

Whites between £5.25 and £6.50

Black Tower Rheinhessen QbA 94   12
(Gilbeys)   *Widely available*
Ripe apple flavours in an easy-drinking off-dry style.

Kendermann Bereich Bernkastel QbA 93   13
(Gilbeys)   *Widely available*
Good crisp fruit. Pleasant acidity and an off-dry finish.

Kendermann Rosenhag Liebfraumilch QbA 94   13
(Gilbeys)   *Widely available*
The wine many of us cut our white wine teeth on! Ripe fruits in an easy-drinking off-dry style.

Piesporter Treppchen Kabinett QmP 93   12
     Quinnsworth
Reminiscent of elderflower on the nose. Low alcohol—7%—so a good choice for lunch and white-meat-based

dishes.

Rudolf Müller Niersteiner Spiegelberg QmP 93 12
Quinnsworth

Spicy floral nose. Lots of ripe fruits on the palate cut through with zesty acidity. Low alcohol.

Sichel QbA 92 11
(Dillons) *Widely available*

Light and lively with good grapefruit flavours, cut through with zesty acidity.

Whites between £6.50 and £8

Deinhard Green Label QbA 93 13
(Gilbeys) *Widely available*

Reliable and consistent. Fresh fruit flavours with crisp acidity ending in an off-dry finish.

Deinhard Riesling Dry QbA 93 12
Mitchells

Steely with a strong floral nose. Good with food.

Dr Heidemann Bernkasteler Badstube Riesling Kabinett QmP 91 14
(Karwig) *Wine merchants/off licences*

Very fresh and aromatic, full of tingling lemon-type acidity with pleasant apple flavours and a long finish.

G. A. Schneider Niersteiner Bildstock Riesling Kabinett QmP 92 14
(Karwig) *Wine merchants/off licences*

Delicate and elegant with its balance between ripe fruit and crisp acidity. All good 'Kabinett' styles should achieve this balance.

Hans Christof Kabinett QmP 93 12
Mitchells

Apples and pears in a fruity yeasty style with good balancing acidity and a short finish.

Rheingau Riesling Trocken QbA 93   12
(Karwig)   *Wine merchants/off licences*
An easy-to-read German wine label! Like biting into a
green apple. Crisp and fresh. A good food wine.

★ **Vier Jahreszeiten Gewürztraminer Kabinett QmP 92** 15
(Karwig)   *Wine merchants/off licences*
Deep golden in colour with deep concentrated floral
aromas and a superb spicy satisfying finish.

Whites between £8 and £10

Dr Wagner Saarburger-Rausch Riesling QbA 92   14
(Karwig)   *Wine merchants/off licences*
A happy balance between low alcohol fruit and acidity.
Perfect summer or apéritif drinking.

**Eitelsbacher Kartauserhofberg Riesling Trocken QbA
89**   14
(Karwig)   *Wine merchants/off licences*
What Riesling in a trocken (dry) style is all about.
Wonderful balance of tingling acidity and floral tones.
Low alcohol makes it a good luncheon wine.

Heritage Range Deinhard Johannisberg QbA 89   13
(Mitchells)   *Wine merchants/off licences*
All the spice, apples and hint of oil that one associates
with quality German winemaking.

Greece

The particularly rich vinous history of ancient Greece has long faded, but accession to the EU may cause a resurgence in interest and may encourage winemakers to make wine with a more international appeal. The first Greek wine to come to mind is Retsina, flavoured with pine resin. Many people, delighted by its flavour while on holiday in the Greek Islands, have been fairly astounded by how poorly it translates into the cooler climate of Western Europe.

The other best-known wines of Greece are Muscat of Pátras, sweet white liqueur wine (Muscat grape); Mavrodaphne of Pátras, sweet red liqueur wine (Mavrodaphne grape); Neméa, full-bodied red wine (Agiorgitiko grape); Náoussa, full-bodied red wine (Xynomavro grape). Côtes de Meliton are red, white and rosé wines from a mixture of native and French varieties. The best-known estate is Château Carras. Muscat of Samos is a well-known sweet dessert Muscat.

Aideen Nolan

WHITE WINES

White under £5.25

★ **Vin de Crete Kourtaki 94**   **15**
(Findlaters)   *Wine merchants/off licences*
Instant appeal with its apple fruit and lively fresh acidity. Deliciously refreshing.

White between £5.25 and £6.50

'Achiaia' Clauss 92   **11**
(Taserra)   *Widely available*
A 'must' for stuffed vine or young cabbage leaves. Good intensity with earthy tones but quite a short finish.

RED WINES

Reds under £5.25

Cava Tsantalis 90   13

Quinnsworth

Very dense ruby colour tones. Rich fruit flavours. Good
structure and tannin.

Kourtaki Vin de Crete 94   13
(Findlaters)   *Wine merchants/off licences*
Wonderful cerise colour. Stewed fruit flavours.

Red between £5.25 and £6.50

'Achaia' Clauss Neméa 90   12
(Taserra)   *Widely available*
Something different: warm raisin-type fruit tones with
just a hint of liquorice.

Red between £10 and £12

★★★**Château Carras 90**   17
(Kevin Parsons)   *Wine merchants/off licences*
Great depth of colour with fruit still closed on aroma.
Fruit attack takes one's breath away. Rich and round
with time to go.

Hungary

A country rich in tradition, Hungary has the most pronounced national character to its wines. Recently outside investors and winemakers have influenced the types of wine produced—for instance, modern clean, fruity Sauvignon and Chardonnay from the Gyöngyös Estate. Hungary also has very interesting indigenous grape varieties, however, and Italian winemakers are paying particular attention to the red Kékfrankos grape. Hungary also has a particular style of sweet wine—Tokaji—unique to itself. Provided that Hungary manages not to lose too much of its individuality, it has plenty of scope to adapt its wines to the international market.

Grape varieties

White: Furmint, Hárslevelü, Szürkebarát, Leányka, Olaszrizling, Ezerjó, Mezesfehér, Sauvignon Blanc, Chardonnay and Pinot Blanc.
Red: Kadarka, Kékfrankos, Pinot Noir, Merlot and more recently Cabernet Sauvignon.

Labels

Wines are named mainly by district name followed by grape name, e.g. Egri Bikaver is Bikaver (Bull's Blood) from the town of Egri. Minosegi Bor is the labelling term for quality wine. Tokaji, that most famous wine, is labelled Szamorodni when more or less dry, Aszú when sweet, and Aszú Eszencia for the sweetest, highest quality of Tokaji.

Aideen Nolan

WHITE WINES

Whites under £5.25

Bataapati Estate Tramini 93   13
(Grants)   *Widely available*
Lots of aroma reminiscent of orange peel. Good acidity
levels and good length.

Chapel Hill Chardonnay 94   13
(Barry & Fitzwilliam)   *Widely available*
Oak influence adds interest to the apple-type fruit
flavours.

White between £6.50 and £8

Disznoko Tokaji Dry Furmint 93   12
(Searsons)   *Wine merchants/off licences*
Don't be put off by the lack of fruit on the nose. A
smoky wine that delivers on fruit, acidity and balance.

RED WINES

Reds under £5.25

Bataapati Estate Kékfrankos 93   12
(Grants)   *Widely available*
Drink slightly cool. A good luncheon wine with smoky
fruits reminiscent of a good Beaujolais.

Chapel Hill 92   11
(Barry & Fitzwilliam)   *Widely available*
Well made, lively and young with hints of liquorice.

[176]

Italy

From a sun-warmed hillside in Tuscany, looking down across tumbling vines to the valley below, still wreathed in swathes of autumnal mist, the medieval stone villages and stark cypress trees seem to float on top of the clouds, much as Renaissance artists pictured them. A few miles away lie the frenetic industrial suburbs of more prosaic Poggibonsi. This juxtaposed landscape could be a metaphor for Italian wine culture.

The contemporary face of Italian wine, at the cutting edge of modern winemaking and now demonstrating equal dedication to viticultural research, draws deeply from the accumulated experience and tradition of ancient and Renaissance worlds.

Vines have been cultivated in Italy since at least Etruscan times (seventh to third centuries BC). Some varieties were brought there by the Phoenicians and the Greeks, who called the country Oenotria, land of vines. Roman legions carried the vine through Gaul right up to Trier in Germany and beyond.

Until recent years, many vineyard practices differed little from that era, based on share-cropping and 'agricoltura promiscua', surely a more romantic notion than mixed farming!

In this century, the ravages of war inhibited development until the 1960s and 1970s. Investment was scarce and there was a philosophy of quantity over quality, cheap and not so cheerful, much destined for the wine lake. Alongside this vinous suicide tendency, however, many old aristocratic families soldiered on, producing superb wine; some, like the Antinori, the Frescobaldi and the Ricasoli, for many centuries. It was the Antinori and their many family branches who spearheaded the quality revolution in the 1970s with wines like Sassicaia and Tignanello. Since then, the innate Italian genius for creativity and design has known no bounds. Their wine industry is now one of the most exciting in the world.

What makes it so exhilarating?

First of all it is the grape varieties. Boredom with ubiquitous Chardonnay and Cabernet makes experimental consumers look for new flavours. These are to be found in bewildering abundance in Italy. For a while it looked as if the Italians, lemming-like, were going to follow blindly the trend towards international varietals, but in the 1990s there has been a sea-change. Whilst most top estates field one or two 'super vini da tavola', almost all are putting their greatest efforts into improving native varieties such as Nebbiolo, Sangiovese, Barbera, Corvina, Negroamaro (red) and Verdicchio, Vernaccia, Garganega and Malvasia (white); even the humble Trebbiano is improving. These wines are full of flavour and character.

The good news is that this push for quality and individuality is happening right across the price categories from noble estates to merchant houses, from small growers to co-operatives. Pride in the product and sheer artistry have taken hold right across the land, from the ultra-traditional Piedmont in the north-west, over to Trentino-Alto Adige and Friuli in the north-east, down through the Veneto to the cradle of change, Tuscany, and on through the heart of the south to the islands of Sicily and Sardinia. Wine is made in every region of Italy.

The best news of all is that Irish importers are breaking with their traditional dismissiveness of Italian wine and are realising that there is treasure trove.

So what to choose?

Labels are poetic but confusing. Some name a village, such as Bardolino. Others name a grape variety and its region of origin, e.g. Brunello di Montalcino, Nebbiolo d'Alba, Montepulciano d'Abruzzo. Others are a single vineyard, like La Poja, Granbussia, etc. Still others are fanciful names such as Tignanello, Coltassala or Ornellaia.

Quality designations

Denominazione di Origine Controllata e Garantita (DOCG): This is the guaranteed very top quality granted only to a handful of regions.

Denominazione di Origine Controllata (DOC): This is the most common designation, similar to AC wines in France.

Indicazione Geografica Tipica (IGT): This is a new category similar to Vin de Pays.

Vino da tavola: Ordinary table wine. However, many top-quality wines have used this category if they fall outside the strict rules of DOC, for instance for using non-local grape varieties. These can usually be spotted by the price, heavy bottle and designer label.

Styles

Big, full-bodied red wines: Suitable for cellaring, but need to be opened to breathe a few hours before use.

   From Piedmont—Barolo, Barbaresco, some Barberas, mainly oak-aged examples.

   From Veneto—Valpolicella Amarone (Corvina, Rondinella, Molinara).

   From Tuscany—Brunello di Montalcino, Vino Nobile di Montepulciano; Riservas from Carmignano; Chianti Classico and Chianti Rufina Riservas (mainly Sangiovese).

   From Umbria—Torgiano (Sangiovese).

   From Campania—Taurasi (Aglianico).

   From Puglia and the islands—most wines made from the Negroamaro and Nero d'Avola grapes such as Salice Salentino.

Earlier drinking wines: Particularly suitable for food, especially Italian cuisine. Nebbiolo d'Alba or Asti; Dolcetto; most Barberas; Valpolicella Superiore (or Ripasso); Cabernet and Merlot and Pinot Nero from the north-east and Emilia Romagna; non-riserva Chianti; Teroldego and Refosco from the north. Rosso Conero and Montepulciano d'Abruzzo are new stars on the market. Also watch for Rossos di Montalcino and Montepulciano.

For light quaffing: Freisa, Grignolino, Valpolicella, Bardolino.

Whites: Most Italian whites are pale, light, very fresh and ideal for matching with food or just sipping. Examples are Arneis, Cortese, Gavi from Piedmont; Soave, Lugana and Bianco di Custoza from Veneto; Chardonnay, Pinot Grigio, Pinot Bianco and Sauvignon Blanc from the north-east and Emilia Romagna; Verdicchio from the Marches; Vernaccia, Trebbiano and Galestro from Tuscany; Malvasia and Grechetto from the south (also found in Frascati, Orvieto and other popular whites). Greco di Tufo from Campania is unusual. However, the barrique has also found its way to Italy and there are some huge oaked Chardonnays around. Top estates usually have one. Some are superb, others heavy-handed.

Italy produces some excellent sparkling wines apart from the vivacious, low-alcohol, refreshing Asti Spumante (Moscato). There are some top-quality Brut styles, many of which rival Champagne. Italian sweet wines are an undiscovered gem: look for good Vin Santo, aged for five years in small barrels called *caratelli*, giving them an oxidised style not unlike Sherry but fruitier. Other *recioto* (late-picked) and semi-dried grapes are used for a wide range of *passito* wines, such as Recioto di Soave (white) and Valpolicella (red), and, of course, one should never forget the famous Marsala, a fortified wine from Sicily. Look for De Bartoli or Pellegrino.

It is impossible to do justice to these wines in a few lines. Italy alternates with France as the biggest wine producer in the world, with over 60m hectolitres per annum produced from 1.4m hectares of vineyard. Take my word for it, go explore!

Monica Murphy

WHITE WINES

Whites under £4.50

Badia Orvieto Classico DOC 94   12

Dunnes Stores

Typical style with nutty overtones and good lingering finish.

Il Casato Soave DOC 94   13

(Ecock)   *Widely available*

A very 'correct' wine. Delivers on fruit and style.

Lamberti Orvieto Classico Secco DOC 93   13

(Gilbeys)   *Widely available*

Dry and balanced. Enhanced with nutty fruit tones.

Whites between £4.50 and £5.25

Castellani Orvieto Classico DOC 94   11

(Cassidy)   *Widely available*

Pleasant and uncomplicated in an easy-drinking style, with a touch of hazelnut.

Miglianico Trebbiano d'Abruzzo DOC 93   12

(Ecock)   *Widely available*

Lively acidity mixes with subtle apple fruits. Ideal party wine.

Sartori Pinot Grigio nv   11

(Cassidy)   *Widely available*

Party wine with easy-drinking appeal. Open and enjoy!

Whites between £5.25 and £6.50

Antinori Orvieto Classico DOC 94   13

(Grants)   *Widely available*

Shows quality wine-making. The fruit is there but it is subtle. Fresh acidity cuts through, leaving a good crisp finish.

Barone Cornacchia Trebbiano d'Abruzzo DOC 94   12
(Karwig)   *Wine merchants/off licences*
Golden in colour, citrus-type aromas and a nutty finish.

Bigi Orvieto Classico Secco DOC 94   13
(Findlaters)   *Wine merchants/off licences*
Fresh and tasty with just the right balance of lively
acidity and fruit.

Cà Donini Pinot Grigio 94   12
(Dillons)   *Widely available*
Garden party wine with its refreshing hint of spritz and
touch of fruit.

Farnese Trebbiano d'Abruzzo DOC 94   13
(Karwig)   *Wine merchants/off licences*
Hints of marzipan. Good fruit development and some
length to the finish.

Masi Soave Classico Superiore DOC 93   14
(Grants)   *Widely available*
The perfect crisp fresh wine with hints of nutty over-
tones.

Pasqua Pinot-Chardonnay Frizzante DOC nv   12
(Woodford Bourne)   *Widely available*
Perfect picnic wine with its easy fruity appeal and
spritzy taste.

Righetti Bianco di Custoza DOC 94   13
(Karwig)   *Wine merchants/off licences*
Very well-made wine with a hint of spritz and delightful
hazelnut tones, particularly on the end.

  Whites between £6.50 and £8

Battaglia Verdicchio dei Castelli di Jesi DOC 94   14
(Findlaters)   *Wine merchants/off licences*
Lively and fresh. A perfect apéritif or good accompani-
ment to fish dishes.

Bersano Gavi DOC 93   13
(Remy)   *Widely available*
Fresh and lively in an uncomplicated style with all the
hallmarks of good winemaking.

Bigi Orvieto Classico 'Torricella' DOC 93/4   14
(Findlaters)   *Wine merchants/off licences*
From a top vineyard site, the wine exhibits a pronounced
grassy aroma and more structure than most.

★★ **Brunori Verdicchio dei Castelli di Jesi DOC 94**   16
                                                    Delitalia
A classy wine and one of the best Verdicchios available.
Nutty overtones with a lively crisp finish that leaves the
palate whistle clean.

★ **Colli di Catone Frascati Superiore DOC 94**   15
(Febvre)   *Widely available*
Distinctive frosted bottle. Produced from 100%
Malvasia. Nutty nuances with a smooth finish mark the
top quality of this wine.

★ **Frescobaldi Albizzia 93**   15
(Allied Drinks)   *Widely available*
Grabs attention with its hints of hazelnuts, good fruit
development on the palate and long finish.

★ **Garofoli Verdicchio dei Castelli di Jesi Classico DOC 93**
                                                         15
(Febvre)   *Widely available*
Excellent creamy fruit character and lively finish.

★ **La Raia Gavi DOC 94**   15
                                                    Delitalia
Produced from the Cortese grape. Light and fresh in an
easy uncomplicated style.

Mezzacorona Moscato Giallo Trentino DOC 93   13
Mitchells
Floral and fruity with lots of Moscato appeal and hints
of marmalade aroma. A perfect apéritif or dessert wine.

Mezzacorona Pinot Grigio Trentino DOC 94   12
Mitchells
Nice ripe peach tones with pleasant crisp acidity and
some length to finish.

Pighin Grave del Friuli Sauvignon DOC 94   13
(Karwig)   *Wine merchants/off licences*
Creamy ripe greengage fruit with a hint of sherbet on
the finish.

**Teruzzo & Puthod Vernaccia di San Gimignano DOC
93**   14
(Karwig/Searsons)   *Wine merchants/off licences*
Light clean fruit and zesty acidity. Nuances of peach
and almond with the creaminess imprinted by good
winemaking techniques. Touch of spice on the finish.

★ **Tiefenbrunner Chardonnay Alto Adige DOC 93**   15
(Karwig/Searsons)   *Wine merchants/off licences*
Glorious Chardonnay without oak influence. Subtle
melon-type fruits and good acidity that combine to end
in a long fruity finish.

Zonin Frascati DOC 93   14
(Valcomino)   *Widely available*
Elegant, with a pleasant touch of hazelnut. Good weight
and structure end in a long finish.

Zonin Soave DOC 93   14
(Valcomino)   *Widely available*
Clean, fresh and lively. Perfect drinking when friends
call.

White between £8 and £10

Avignonesi Chardonnay/Sauvignon 93   13
(Karwig)   *Wine merchants/off licences*
Almonds and nougat with quite a fat texture and good
spicy finish.

Whites between £10 and £12

Carpineto Farnito Chardonnay 93   13
(Taserra)   *Widely available*
Super subtle toasty aromas which carry through on
flavour, backed up with fresh acidity and a long elegant
finish.

Carpineto Querciabella Orvieto Classico Secco DOC 93
(Taserra)   *Widely available*   13
Pale gold in colour with subtle marzipan and nutty
aromas. Oak-influenced. Fans out on the palate with
good length, balanced acidity and a hint of spice on the
finish.

Lageder Chardonnay DOC 94   14
(Febvre)   *Wine merchants/off licences*
Subtle use of oak imparts character to this very well-
made wine with apple-type fruits and tingling fresh
acidity.

Lageder Pinot Grigio DOC 94   14
(Febvre)   *Wine merchants/off licences*
Good example of this style. Full of slight nutty tones
with a lingering, elegant finish.

Le Monde Pinot Grigio DOC 94   13
          Delitalia
Vibrant with subtle fruit character. A clean fresh finish.

White between £12 and £15

★★**Antinori Cervaro della Salla 93**   16
(Grants)   *Wine merchants/off licences*
Balanced and harmonious. The Chardonnay grape

imparts peach and apple-like fruit, and the oak gives an elegant and subtle finish which needs time to show its promise.

RED WINES

Reds under £4.50

★ **Arietta Montepulciano d'Abruzzo DOC 94**   15
Quinnsworth

Enjoyable dark chocolate aromas with a delicious bite of ripe fruit backed up with good balancing acidity. Note the pleasant bitter twist on the finish.

Gallico Valpolicella DOC nv   13
Dunnes Stores

Deep crimson in colour with a typical bitter-sweet fruit effect. Easy-drinking in an uncomplicated style.

Il Casato Merlot nv   12
Ecock

Ruby red with a stalky pungent aroma. Flavours fan out into pepper and spices making it a good choice with food.

Il Casato Valpolicella DOC 94   13
Ecock

Lots of cherry fruit with a good bite of acidity make great easy drinking.

Reds between £4.50 and £5.25

Augusto Valpolicella DOC nv   11
(Dillons)   *Widely available*
Cold tea aromas with chocolate and cherry flavours. Easy-drinking style.

Castellani Chianti DOCG 93   12
(Cassidy)   *Widely available*
Appetising bitter-sweet fruit flavours with quite a short finish.

Cecchi Chianti DOCG 94   13
Quinnsworth

Light ruby in colour. Has the sweet chocolate cherry
flavours that are the hallmarks of well-produced
Chianti.

Miglianico Montepulciano d'Abruzzo DOC 94   14
Ecock

Good brambly fruit with a delicious bite of acidity and
clean, fresh, fruity finish. Well rounded with a long
satisfying finish.

Reds between £5.25 and £6.50

Araldica Barbera d'Asti Superiore DOC 92   13
(Findlaters)   *Wine merchants/off licences*
Intense plummy fruit appeal and soft lively finish. Just
right after a hard day.

Araldica Dolcetto d'Asti DOC 93   12
(Findlaters)   *Wine merchants/off licences*
Easy to drink with lots of spice, red berry fruits and a
nice bite of acidity.

★ **Badia Alle Corti Chianti Classico Riserva 90**   15
Dunnes Stores

Lively cherry fruit flavours fan out on the palate. A
pleasant bitter-sweet tone combines with harmonious
tannins to leave a long finish.

Barone Cornacchia Montepulciano d'Abruzzo DOC 93
(Karwig)   *Widely available*   14
Deep cerise in colour. The bite of ripe fruit flavours is
overlain with hints of liquorice. Pronounced acidity
makes this a food wine.

Bolla Bardolino Classico DOC 93   12
(Dillons)   *Widely available*
Meant for party time! Serve cool and note the hint of
spritz.

Conti Serristori Chianti DOCG 93   11
(Dillons)   *Widely available*
Easy-drinking Chianti. Serving cool will help to enhance
the fruit flavours.

Farnese Montepulciano d'Abruzzo DOC 93   14
(Karwig)   *Widely available*
Dried fruit aromas and flavours. A great chewy mouthful of wine which ends in a chocolate fruit liqueur
finish.

Masi Valpolicella Classico Superiore DOC 93   13
(Grants)   *Widely available*
Pleasant attack of bitter-sweet fruit backed up with
balancing acidity.

Reds between £6.50 and £8

Bersano Barbera d'Asti DOC 92   14
(Remy)   *Wine merchants/off licences*
More concentrated fruit flavours than most Barbera
d'Asti. Will delight with its plummy fruit and appealing
easy finish.

Bersano Dolcetto d'Alba DOC 92   14
(Remy)   *Wine merchants/off licences*
Blackberry in colour with lots of tangy ripe fruits and a
delicious bite of acidity.

Candido Salice Salentino Riserva DOC 90   14
(Findlaters)   *Wine merchants/off licences*
A wine with attitude! Full of spice, cherry fruit with a
big hearty finish.

★**Colle Secco Montepulciano d'Abruzzo DOC 92**   15
(Febvre)   *Widely available*
Morello cherry aromas which carry through on flavour
end in a nice bite of fruit.

[189   ]

Conti Serristori Chianti Classico DOCG 92   13
(Dillons)   *Widely available*
Cherry in colour and in flavour with a pleasant bitter
chocolate finish.

★ **Frescobaldi Remole Chianti DOCG 93**   15
(Allied Drinks)   *Widely available*
Wild and wonderful Chianti with lots of cherry/
chocolate flavours ending in an impressive finish.

★ **Le Pergole Vino Nobile di Montepulciano DOCG 90**   15
                                       Dunnes Stores
Hearty and full-bodied. Garnet with tile brick reflections.
Black cherry and chocolate flavours followed by a
pleasant bitter twist.

Mezzacorona Teroldego Rotaliano DOC 92   14
                                       Mitchells
Produced from the Teroldego grape. Classy 'chunky'
wine that pulls all the elements of taste together.

Pighin Grave del Friuli Merlot DOC 93   12
(Karwig)   *Wine merchants/off licences*
Stalky fruit nose with a good sweet attack and surprising
amount of tannin giving a slightly bitter finish.

★ **Rocca delle Macie Chianti Classico Riserva DOCG 90** 15
(Searsons/Febvre)   *Widely available*
Rich bitter-sweet fruit jumps out of the glass. Combined
with lively acidity, gives perfect drinking pleasure.

Sartori Grave del Friuli Merlot DOC 93   12
(Cassidy)   *Widely available*
Pungent tones with stalky red berry fruit make this a
good food wine.

Teruzzi & Puthod Peperino 93   13
(Karwig)   *Wine merchants/off licences*
Extra heavy brown bottle. Bite of liquorice—good
development and a long luscious finish.

★ **Vigneti di Montupoli Montepulciano d'Abruzzo DOC 92**
Ecock 15

Very appealing, with an intriguing bitter chocolate
flavour. Enticing is the word.

★ **Villa Cerna Chianti Classico Riserva DOCG 91** 15
Quinnsworth

Not for the faint-hearted. Cherry fruit with a kick-back
of drying tannins and a delicious bite of acidity.

Reds between £8 and £10

★ **Antinori Chianti Classico Riserva DOCG 90/91** 15
(Grants) *Widely available*
Excellent intense cherry fruits with a delicious bite of
dark chocolate on the finish. Very appealing.

Avignonesi Rosso di Montepulciano DOC 92 13
(Karwig) *Wine merchants/off licences*
The tar, leather and liquorice aromas of this wine give
way to a smack of ripe fruits which linger and finish in a
pleasantly austere style.

Avignonesi Vino Nobile di Montepulciano DOCG 91
(Searsons) *Widely available* 14
Beautifully mature with a big sweet fruit attack and long
flavoursome finish.

Badia a Coltibuono Chianti Classico DOCG 91 14
(Findlaters) *Widely available*
Top example of Chianti Classico with plenty of cherry
fruit flavours and a pleasant bitter twist to the finish.

Bersano Barolo DOCG 91 13
(Remy) *Wine merchants/off licences*
Brick in colour with a base of chocolate and liquorice
aromas and flavours rounded out by high acidity.

★★**Castello di Nipozzano Chianti Rufina Riserva DOCG 91** 17
(Allied Drinks) *Widely available*
Has all the Chianti characteristics—cherry and chocolate

[191]

with a rich savoury finish. Wonderful drinking.

★ **Feyles Barbera d'Alba DOC 90** 15
Delitalia

Barbera grape imparts firm tannins, dense concentrated
fruit reminiscent of figs and prunes and a deep saturation
of colour.

★ **Il Poggione Rosso di Montalcino DOC 93** 15
Delitalia

Produced from the Sangiovese grape. A real stunner.
Layers of rich ripe fruits end in a pleasant bitter twist.

Lungarotti Rubesco DOC 91 13
(Findlaters) *Wine merchants/off licences*
From Torgiano in Central Italy. Tasty bite of cherry with
a mineral back-bone.

★ **Notarpanaro Rosso del Salento Vino da Tavola 85** 15
Ecock

Lots of vanilla and coffee aromas with impressive fruit
flavours that carry right through to the finish.

★ **Ruffino Chianti Classico Riserva DOCG 90** 15
(Dillons) *Widely available*
Top-quality wine with instant appeal. Smooth in texture
with nutty overtones. Impressive finish, rich in flavour
and style.

★ **Santo Stefano Vino di Ripasso 90** 15
(Febvre) *Wine merchants/off licences*
Great depth of flavour with tangy black cherry, mouth-
watering acidity and tannin combine in a voluptuous
finish.

★**Taurino Salice Salentino Riserva DOC 90** 15
Ecock

Mature and complex with smooth fruit and a streak of
tobacco. Big and beefy.

Reds between £10 and £12

★ **Bolla Amarone Recioto della Valpolicella DOC 86**   15
(Dillons)   *Wine merchants/off licences*
Produced from naturally dried grapes. Concentrated
flavours and a rich ripe finish. A big port-like wine.

★ **Carpineto Chianti Classico Riserva DOCG 90**   15
(Taserra)   *Widely available*
Rich ripe Sangiovese. Oak influenced with smooth
tannins and a bite of cherry on the long finish.

Carpineto Farnito Cabernet Sauvignon 91   14
(Taserra)   *Widely available*
Deep cherry in colour. Spicy flavours with hints of
nutmeg ending in a creamy finish.

Carpineto Vino Nobile di Montepulciano DOCG 89   13
(Taserra)   *Widely available*
Deep ruby in colour. Some 'soapy' aromas with a hint of
liquorice. Flavours open up on the palate and end in a
smooth lingering finish.

★ **Garofoli Rosso Conero Riserva Agontano DOC 90**   15
(Febvre)   *Wine merchants/off licences*
Silky texture, chocolate overtones and appetising chewy
fruit.

Reds between £12 and £15

★ **Fontanafredda Barolo di Serralunga d'Alba DOCG 90**   15
(Karwig)   *Wine merchants/off licences*
An interesting wine in an interesting bottle! Orange-
tinted. Packed tight with cherry and dark chocolate
flavours. The big attack of bitter-sweet fruit is cut
through by a high note of acidity.

La Caduta Rosso di Montalcino DOC 92   14
(Febvre)   *Widely available*
Youthful with good juicy fruit and pleasant supple
finish.

[193   ]

★★ **Masi Campo Fiorin Amarone della Valpolicella DOC
91**   16
(Grants)   *Widely available*
Extremely rich and powerful! Laced with chewy fruit
concentration in a rich port-like style.

★ **Monte Calvi Greve Vino da Tavola 92**   15
(Parsons)   *Wine merchants/off licences*
Super Tuscan from a mediocre vintage. Dense cherry
tones overlain with aromas of shoe-leather. Worth the
money if you're looking for something different.

Reds between £15 and £20

★ **Antinori Tignanello DOC 91**   15
(Grants)   *Widely available*
The quality revolution started here! One of the original
super Tuscans—now DOC. Classic style with smoky
aromas and dense cherry fruits. Produced from 80%
Sangiovese and 20% Cabernet Sauvignon.

★ **Carpineto Brunello di Montalcino DOCG 90**   15
(Taserra)   *Widely available*
Tile brick in colour with orange highlights. Ageing in
oak adds a spicy bite to the sweet dark chocolate and
cherry fruit. Smooth with good structure and high
alcohol.

Red between £20 and £30

Pio Cesare Barolo DOCG 91   16
                                                              Findlaters
★★ A very distinctive wine—powerful and concentrated,
needing time to show its greatness. Tight-knit complex
spicy tones wrap around fruit and high acidity. Flavours
last long after the last swallow.

New Zealand

New Zealand's long narrow shape, and two main islands,
North Island and South Island, mean that its vineyards
are never more than 80 miles from the sea. They benefit
from clear sunlight and are cooled at night by sea breezes.
In the 1980s wines made from Sauvignon Blanc firmly
established the country's reputation, followed closely by
those made from Chardonnay.

WHITE WINES

Whites between £6.50 and £8

Cooks Hawkes Bay Chardonnay 92   12
(Allied Drinks)   *Widely available*
Hints of banana with a distinguishing stamp of zesty
acidity.

Montana Chardonnay 94   14
(Grants)   *Widely available*
Cool crisp Chardonnay with just a hint of pineapple and
crisp acidity.

❦ **Montana Marlborough Sauvignon Blanc 95**   15
(Grants)   *Widely available*
Super example of New Zealand Sauvignon Blanc.
Gooseberries and nettles with a twist of lemon juice
acidity.

Morton Estate Hawkes Bay Chardonnay 94   14
(Dillons)   *Widely available*
Good fruit with a slight hint of kiwi. Long, lingering
crisp finish.

Morton Estate Hawkes Bay Sauvignon Blanc 94   13
(Dillons)   *Widely available*
Packed with grassy, herbaceous nutty aromas. Lively
lemon-type acidity leaves a crisp finish.

Whites between £8 and £10

Aotea Chardonnay 94   13
(Kevin Parsons)   *Wine merchants/off licences*
Aotearoa is the Maori name for New Zealand. Ripe
exotic Chardonnay fruit tones. Good structure, depth of
flavour and finish.

Aotea Sauvignon Blanc 94   14
(Kevin Parsons)   *Wine merchants/off licences*
An excellent example of just how good Sauvignon Blanc
can be.

Hawkes Bay Morton Estate Chardonnay 94   13
(Dillons)   *Widely available*
Big, up-front tropical fruit flavours. Good with food.

Matua Valley Sauvignon Blanc 93   14
(Woodford Bourne)   *Widely available*
Deep green/gold in colour with the pungency of nettles.
Ripe fruit and good acidity give a refreshing finish.

Rothbury Estate Sauvignon Blanc 92   13
(Woodford Bourne)   *Widely available*
Has all the appeal of good herbaceous fruit ending in a
lively finish.

Seifried Estate Riesling Dry 93   13
(Kevin Parsons)   *Wine merchants/off licences*
Zesty limey acidity, good alcohol. Pleasant tropical fruit
tones.

Stoneleigh Marlborough Sauvignon Blanc/Chardonnay 93
(Allied Drinks)   *Widely available*   14
Tingling fresh acidity, crisp apple flavours and long
finish.

Whites between £10 and £12

Babich Hawkes Bay Sauvignon Blanc 94 13
Mitchells

Definite stewed gooseberry fruits with intense lively
acidity and succulent long finish.

Hawkes Bridge Sauvignon Blanc 94 14
(Kevin Parsons) *Wine merchants/off licences*
Good gooseberry tones with flavours that fan out.
Elegant long finish.

★**Hunter's Chardonnay 92** 15
(Gilbeys) *Widely available*
Delightful and delicious with oak influence imparting
peach-like tones, held together with a crisp lively
acidity.

★**Hunter's Sauvignon Blanc 94** 16
(Gilbeys) *Widely available*
A star, with its brilliant balance of creamy gooseberry
fruit and citrus acidity. Fruit and excellent length of
flavour add class.

★**Redwood Valley Sauvignon Blanc 93** 15
(Kevin Parsons) *Wine merchants/off licences*
Superb New Zealand Sauvignon with complex grassy
tones and great depth of flavour. Excellent.

★**Wairau River Sauvignon Blanc 94** 15
Terroirs

A real charmer. Nettles on aroma but gooseberry fruit
fans out on the palate and is shot through with very
lively but not tart acidity. Great length.

White between £15 and £20

★**Cloudy Bay Chardonnay 94** 15
(Findlaters) *Wine merchants/off licences*
A rich combination of ripe grapefruit tones with smoky
oak. Superb balance ending in a toasty subtle finish.

RED WINES

Red between £6.50 and £8

Montana Cabernet Sauvignon 95   12
(Grants)   *Widely available*
Cabernet Sauvignon from New Zealand tends to be on
the lean side. Pea-pod aroma. Good with food.

Reds between £8 and £10

Hawkes Bay Morton Estate Cabernet/Merlot 93   12
(Dillons)   *Wine merchants/off licences*
Vegetal tones reminiscent of runner beans. Another
good food wine.

Matua Cabernet Sauvignon/Merlot 92   13
(Woodford Bourne)   *Wine merchants/off licences*
Spicy with a damp earth tone typical of New Zealand.

Stoneleigh Cabernet Sauvignon 92   14
(Allied Drinks)   *Widely available*
Aged in French oak. Typical New Zealand style—more
herbaceous than fruity, so needs food.

Red between £12 and £15

Hawkes Bay Vidal Cabernet Sauvignon/Merlot 93   14
(Kevin Parsons)   *Wine merchants/off licences*
Cabernet Sauvignon dominates slightly. Characteristic
pea-pod aroma. Good example of this style.

Portugal

The wine revolution that followed Portugal's accession to the EU in 1986 is likely to have a far more significant effect on Portugal's economic development than the political revolution which preceded it.

In the past, wines were mainly made for, and drunk by, the Portuguese themselves. The reds (80 per cent of production) were harsh and tannic, with fading fruit from prolonged cask ageing. The whites were dull, fruitless and often oxidised. The main exports were the rosé brands of Mateus and Lancers and some white Vinho Verde. Now, thanks to EU funding and new legislation, great strides have been made. Value-for-money, modern, clean styles are appearing and a big export drive is under way.

Portugal's great strength is in its wealth of indigenous grape varieties, particularly Touriga Nacional, Baga and Castelão Francês. The use of stainless steel and temperature controlled fermentation is giving whites a new-found flavour and freshness, and reds are balanced, with rich fruit and oaky tones.

Unfortunately, in an industry dominated by co-operatives, many winemakers are still very slow to progress. However, a handful of producers have broken the traditional, conservative mould, resulting in the upgrading of co-operatives at Almerim, Arruda and Borba, for example. The independent Sogrape company has invested heavily in the Douro, Dão and Bairrada regions, and Australian winemaker David Baverstock has been turning out top-quality wines from the Esporão estate in Alentejo. Setúbal-based José Maria da Fonseca and J. P. Vinhos have bought vineyards in Alentejo, producing the popular Tinto Velho and Tinto da Anfora, respectively.

The recent introduction of the Indicação de Proveniência Regulamentada (IPR) category brought many new areas in line for Denominação de Origem Controlada (DOC) promotion, and the new Vinho Regional category is similar to the French Vin de Pays.

Progress may be slow in Portugal but, for the forward-thinking producer, there is great potential.

Main regions

Vinho Verde: North-west, temperate, granite soil, vines trained high.

Douro: North-east along Douro river valley, hot summers, cold wet winters, granite and schist, steep terraced vineyards.

Dão: Central location, temperate—severe winter temperatures.

Bairrada: Atlantic coastal area, oceanic climate, clay soil.

Oeste: North of Lisbon, rolling hilly countryside, limestone soil.

Ribatejo: Flat alluvial plains along Tagus valley.

Setúbal Peninsula: South of Lisbon, limestone and sandy soil.

Alentejo: Near Spanish border, undulating plains of granite and schist, very hot summer temperatures—little rainfall.

Grape varieties

White: Alvarinho, Arinto, Fernão Pires, Loureiro, Moscatel, Roupeiro.

Red: Baga, Bastardo, Castelão Francês (Periquita), Tinta Pinheira, Tinta Roriz, Touriga Nacional.

Styles

White: Fresh, crisp and fruity with lemony acidity, to be drunk young. Typical white Vinho Verde is dry/off-dry, with moderate alcohol and an aromatic refreshing spritzy finish.

Red: Ranges from up-front fruity styles with supple tannins for early drinking, through tannic styles that need time to balance, to *garrafeira*, which is very mature and spicy with vanilla-like characteristics.

Rosé: Medium dry, light, slightly pétillant table wine for early consumption.

Sparkling: Similar in style to Champagne.

Producers

Co-operatives buy grapes from farmers. Large independent merchants produce branded and own-label wines. Single quinta/estate—small private producer.

Quality status

Denominação de Origem Controlada (DOC): Quality wine.
Indicação de Proveniência Regulamentada (IPR): Similar to Vin Délimité de Qualité Supérieure.
Vinho Regional: Similar to Vin de Pays.
Vinho de Mesa: Table wine.

Labels

Selo de Origem: Numbered seal or origin on quality wines.
Reserva: Wines of superior vintage quality.
Garrafeira: Same as reserva—aged for a longer period in cask and bottle.

Adega: Winery.
Branco: White.
Bruto: Sparkling.
Casta: Grape variety.

Doce: Sweet.
Seco: Dry.
Tinto: Red.
Vinho: Wine.

Catherine Griffith

WHITE WINES

Whites under £4.50

J. P. Branco nv   **14**
(Reynolds)   *Widely available*
Orange and peach aromas with silky fruit flavours and a good crisp finish. Value for money.

Ramada 94 12
Dunnes Stores

Pale yellow with just a hint of apple aromas. Dry with a crisp finish. Easy-drinking style.

Whites between £4.50 and £5.25

Casal Garcia DOC nv 12
Dunnes Stores

Typical light Vinho Verde style with green apple fruit appeal. High acidity and a hint of spritz make it a good wine with fish. Low alcohol.

Mateus White nv 13
(Dillons) *Widely available*

Spritzy refreshing appeal. Well made.

Quinta da Aveleda Vinho Verde DOC nv 12
(Reynolds) *Widely available*

Mildly aromatic with typical hint of spritz. Good fruity attack but high acidity takes over the finish. Perfect with grilled oily fish.

Terra Franca 91 14
(Dillons) *Widely available*

Traditional style with generous greengage fruit that lingers on the finish.

Whites between £5.25 and £6.50

Fonseca Albis 93 12
Mitchells

Lots of grapey aromas reminiscent of Muscat. Pleasant nutmeg overtones with a spicy finish. Perfect apéritif wine.

Grao Vasco Dão DOC 94 13
(Searsons) *Widely available*

Well-balanced with good fruit attack in a crisp clean style. A lively white wine with lemon appeal.

Herdade do Esporão Vinha da Defesa 93 14
(Reynolds) *Widely available*
Refreshing lemon-type acidity backed up with good
apple-type fruits.

Mateus Signature Douro DOC 94 13
(Dillons) *Widely available*
Clean, fresh, well made. Good fruit and acidity balance.

Monte Velho Reguengos 94 14
(Reynolds) *Widely available*
Good intense aromas of peach and apricot with lively
acidity and refreshing finish.

Trajadura da Aveleda 94 12
(Reynolds) *Widely available*
Light and refreshing with a hint of spritz on the palate.
Nice bite of citrus acidity.

Whites between £6.50 and £8

★ **João Pires Branco nv** 15
(Reynolds) *Widely available*
Good balance between fruit and acidity. The delicious
hints of tangy peach on the aroma carry through in
flavour.

Quinta do Carmo 94 14
(Reynolds) *Widely available*
Golden in colour with tropical fruit tones. Medium
length on the finish.

RED WINES

Red under £4.50

J. P. Tinto nv 13
(Reynolds) *Widely available*
Great depth of colour, lots of fruit flavours with reason-
able length on the finish. Good value.

Reds between £4.50 and £5.25

★ **Aliança Bairrada DOC 94**   15
(Reynolds)   *Widely available*
Portugal at its best. Lots of meaty aromas and flavours
backed up with firm tannins. A good food wine.

Aliança Dão DOC 89   12
(Reynolds)   *Widely available*
Deep crimson in colour and full of spicy plummy fruit.

★ **Charamba Douro DOC 92**   15
(Reynolds)   *Widely available*
Amazing quality for the price. Super colour, great fruity
taste. Excellent food wine.

Porta dos Cavaleiros Dão DOC 88   13
(Reynolds)   *Widely available*
Very dense in colour with terracotta tones. Cold tea
aromas. Packs a punch of fruit backed up with tannin
and acidity. Not for the faint-hearted. Drinking well
now.

Reds between £5.25 and £6.50

Aliança Alabastro 92   14
(Reynolds)   *Widely available*
Deep crimson in colour with hints of liquorice and
caramel on the nose. Good length of flavour.

Grao Vasco Dão DOC 92   13
(Searsons)   *Widely available*
Strawberry fruits with chewy tannins and a streak of
acidity. Good food wine.

José Maria da Fonseca Periquita DOC 91   14
(Mitchells)   *Widely available*
A big mouthful of satisfying cherry fruits showing good
structure and character.

Mateus Signature Douro DOC 91   13
(Dillons)   *Widely available*
Plenty of fruit and balance in this wine. An example of
good winemaking.

Monte Velho Reguengos 92   13
(Reynolds)   *Widely available*
Pale ruby in colour with an aroma reminiscent of cold
tea.

Reds between £6.50 and £8

Aliança Dão Reserva DOC 92   14
(Reynolds)   *Widely available*
Bright crimson in colour. Plummy fruits end in a long
satisfying finish.

Aliança Foral Garrafeira 90   14
(Reynolds)   *Widely available*
Lots of red berry fruit and a smooth finish. 'Garrafeira'
means extra ageing which adds complexity.

Quinta de Camarate Fonseca 89   14
                                                       Mitchells
Cabernet Sauvignon and the native Castelão Francês
combine to produce a complex tar and cedar aroma.

Reds between £8 and £10

★ **Esporão Reserva 91**   15
(Reynolds)   *Wine merchants/off licences*
Intense colours with sweet red berry fruit attack followed
by an attractive lush finish.

★ **Tinto Velho 87**   15
                                                       Mitchells
A big wine in every sense—with a wonderful combination of fruit and tannin. Full-bodied with a long mature
finish.

Red between £10 and £12

Quinta do Carmo 88   14
(Reynolds)   *Widely available*
Part-owned by Domaine Baron de Rothschild. Complex
style marked by good red berry fruits, spice and rich
tannins.

ROSÉ WINES

Rosé under £5.25

Mateus Rosé nv   13
(Dillons)   *Widely available*
Memories of youth! Approachable, spritzy, garden
party wine.

Romania

A country with one of the oldest wine histories and the greatest acreage under vine, much of Romania's wine is for home consumption. Privatisation is now under way and advancing technology, increased investment and quite sophisticated labelling laws ensure Romanian wine a growing place on the world market. Rapidly improving white and some excellent sweet white wines offer great value for money. Watch out for some good reds, particularly Pinot Noir from the Dealul Mare region.

Main regions

Cotnari, Murfatlar, Dealul Mare, Tîrnave.

Grape varieties

White: Welschriesling, Sauvignon Blanc, Gewürztraminer and the indigenous Feteasca Alba.

Red: Cabernet Sauvignon, Merlot, Pinot Noir and the indigenous Feteasca Neagra.

Labels

VS: Superior Quality. *VSO:* Superior Quality with Appellation of Origin. *VSOC:* Top of the range with three quality categories—CMD (late harvest); CMI (late harvest with noble rot); CIB (selected late harvest with noble rot).   *Aideen Nolan*

WHITE WINE

White under £5.25

Classic Sauvignon Blanc 92   12
(Barry & Fitzwilliam)   *Widely available*
A party wine. Fresh fruit, medium acidity, a short finish.

RED WINE

Red under £5.25

Classic Pinot Noir 90   13
(Barry & Fitzwilliam)   *Widely available*
Pleasant jammy fruit tones carry through in flavour.

Romanian Mystery

The mystery of Romania is how they have kept secret the magic of their wines for so long. Their secret is finally out.

Cabernet Sauvignon Special Reserve
Rated 'Outstanding'
Wine Magazine January 1995.
'One of those wines that leave you stunned.'
Tom Doorley, *Sunday Tribune* July 1995
'It is a beaut—don't delay.'
Megabites, *The Irish Times*, July 1995

Classic Pinot Noir
'One of the most wonderful Pinot Noirs in the world.'
Oz Clarke *BBC Food and Wine Programme*.
'Classic Pinot Noir is a great mouthful.'
Tom Doorley *Sunday Tribune* July 1995
'This example is impressive—it has very good concentrated fruit.'
Sandy O'Byrne, *The Irish Times*

Other outstanding Romanian wines include:
Merlot Special Edition
Murfatlar Cabernet Sauvignon
Murfatlar Chardonnay
Classic Sauvignon

Imported by **Barry & Fitzwilliam Ltd**
Cork and Dublin.

South Africa

Though considered to be a 'New World' country, South Africa has a longer wine tradition than many countries, its first wine having been made in 1661. Indeed, some of its wines were highly prized in Europe in the eighteenth century, well before many of today's famous French wines were even established. However, history conspired to prevent South Africa making any real impact until recently.

The father of Cape wine was a Dutchman, Jan van Riebeeck. While the Dutch were not great viticulturalists, the fine Constantia estate was founded by a Dutchman in 1685. Thereafter the main influences came from the influx of French Huguenots in 1688 and German settlers in the first half of the twentieth century.

The repeal of the preferential Empire tariffs in 1861 and the onset of phylloxera in 1886 caused great devastation. Replanting with high-yielding varietals such as Cinsaut led to gross over-production. The formation of the KWV in 1918 was meant to improve the situation, but instead made matters worse by effectively removing any quality incentive. Finally, the introduction of apartheid led to sanctions and international alienation.

Thus the wine industry found itself lacking in expertise and experience when sanctions were removed in the early 1990s. By then countries such as Australia and Chile had become serious producers on the world market.

Over the last few years a tremendous effort has been made to improve the image and quality of South African wines and already there are promising results. Better use of new ideas in both viticulture and vinification means that the quality of the wines continues to improve, while greater use of well-known varietals gives South African wines a stronger chance of competing on the international market.

Chenin Blanc, also known as Steen, is still the most

common varietal and is used to make a wide range of styles from clean and crisp to off-dry and bland. Given the hot climate, it is unusual that so much white wine is produced. Unfortunately, South African winemaking has tended to produce overly neutral whites. This is beginning to change with the use of better-known varietals such as Chardonnay and Sauvignon Blanc, with Chardonnay performing well.

Reds are generally made in the French style, and the Bordeaux-style wines are usually excellent. Single Cabernets and Merlots are good. South Africa can boast its own specific varietal—Pinotage, a cross between the Pinot Noir and Cinsaut red grape varieties. These wines have generally been made in a very dull fashion, but there are now some really superb examples emerging. Pinot Noir has great potential in the cooler regions, while Shiraz is fairly popular. All in all, a lot to look forward to over the next few years.

Area under vine

116,000 hectares (Australia 61,000, Germany 107,000, Chile 60,000). 30% Chenin Blanc.

Wine production

10m hectolitres, of which 85% white, 15% red, 51% table wines, 49% fortified wines or brandy. Co-operatives produce 85% of the total crop: 25% becomes wine, 75% becomes grape juice, distilling wine or industrial alcohol.

Annual consumption

8.9 litres per capita in 1992, down from 11.6 litres in 1970.

Exports

Approximately 20% of production is exported; at the end of sanctions this figure was only 5%. Already South Africa has overtaken both New Zealand and Chile in the UK market.

Climate

Generally hot and dry, with some regions having annual rainfall of only 250mm and daily temperatures in the growing season of 23°C, with 40°C in some areas. Newer regions in the extreme south benefit from a maritime climate.

Dermot Nolan

WHITE WINES

White under £4.50

Helderberg Dry White nv 11
Quinnsworth
Fresh subtle fruit aromas in an easy-to-drink style.

Whites between £4.50 and £5.25

Culemborg Chenin Blanc 94 13
Dunnes Stores
Firm fruit tones with a hint of peach and lively acidity. Good length on the finish.

Firgrove Chenin Blanc nv 13
(Barry & Fitzwilliam) *Widely available*
Clean, fresh and fruity with an edge of crisp acidity.

Helderberg Chardonnay 94 14
Quinnsworth
'Lemon peel' is perfect to describe this well-made wine.

★Helderberg Sauvignon Blanc 94 15
Quinnsworth
Superb grassy Sauvignon Blanc aroma. Good attack of fruit and flavour development in a classic style.

Hippo Creek Chenin Blanc 94 13
(Allied Drinks) *Widely available*
Easy-drinking with generous ripe exotic fruit tones and balancing acidity.

Kathenberg Chenin Blanc 94   13
(Greenhills)   *Widely available*
Not much aroma but good fruit in an easy-drinking
style with reasonable length.

Kathenberg Sauvignon Blanc 94   12
(Greenhills)   *Widely available*
Fruitier style of Sauvignon Blanc with quite a broad
flavour and short finish.

KWV Roodeberg Blanc 94   12
(Fitzgeralds)   *Widely available*
Straightforward, well-made wine. Fresh fruit character,
good mouth texture and a hint of spice on the finish.

Van Riebeeck Chenin Blanc 94   13
(Fitzgeralds)   *Widely available*
Another fruity Chenin cut through with tangy acidity.

Van Riebeeck Sauvignon Blanc 94   12
(Fitzgeralds)   *Widely available*
Easy-drinking style. Good choice for a large party.

Villiera Estate Blue Ridge Blanc 94   12
(Grants)   *Widely available*
Nutty and ripe on the palate, good acidity and some
length on the finish.

Whites between £5.25 and £6.50

Drostdy-Hof Steen 94   12
(Febvre)   *Wine merchants/off licences*
Fresh fruity flavours and a medium long finish.

Goedverwacht Estate Colombard 94   12
(Ecock)   *Widely available*
Not much aroma but delivers on fruit flavour. Crisp
acidity gives a balanced finish.

Goedverwacht Estate Sauvignon Blanc 94   11
(Ecock)   *Widely available*
Lots of fruity aromas and flavours make for pleasant
and easy drinking.

Hippo Creek Sauvignon Blanc 94   13
(Allied Drinks)   *Widely available*
Hints of gooseberry with fresh lively acidity give overall
balance.

KWV Chardonnay 94   13
(Fitzgeralds)   *Wine merchants/off licences*
Easy-drinking style of ripe, peach-like Chardonnay.

KWV Chenin Blanc 94   13
(Fitzgeralds)   *Wine merchants/off licences*
Tangy apple aromas that carry through on flavour with
balanced acidity and good weighty finish. Makes a good
apéritif.

KWV Sauvignon Blanc/Chardonnay 94   13
(Fitzgeralds)   *Wine merchants/off licences*
Sauvignon dominates, though the pleasant apple
characteristics of Chardonnay come through. Good fruit
development with considerable length to the finish.

Nederburg Chardonnay 93   13
(Dillons)   *Widely available*
Limited oak maturation adds complexity. Appealing
peach-like fruit with a silky texture.

Nederburg Sauvignon Blanc/Chardonnay 93   11
(Dillons)   *Widely available*
Sauvignon imparts the herbal tone and Chardonnay the
ripe apple fruits. Easy drinking.

Simonsig Sauvignon Blanc 94   12
(United Beverages)   *Widely available*
Easy-drinking white. Perfect for a large party.

Whites between £6.50 and £8

Bellingham Blancenberger nv   12
Dunnes Stores
Sauvignon Blanc and Chenin Blanc combine to produce
a pleasant lively wine with a hint of spritz.

Cardouw Sauvignon Blanc 93   11
(Woodford Bourne)   *Widely available*
Fresh and fruity in an easy-drinking style.

Fleur du Cap Chardonnay 94   14
(Febvre)   *Widely available*
Classic oak-matured Chardonnay. Subtle creamy oak
influence backing up the fruit. Ends with a hint of spice.

Hippo Creek Chardonnay 93   13
(Allied Drinks)   *Widely available*
Oak influence adds subtle butterscotch tones. Leaving it
on its lees adds structure and complexity.

Two Oceans Sauvignon Blanc 95   13
(Febvre)   *Widely available*
Refreshing floral aromas backed up with a mouthful of
good fruit and crisp acidity.

RED WINES

Reds under £4.50

Helderberg Cinsaut/Shiraz 94   13
Quinnsworth
Hints of eucalyptus with good fruit attack. A soft centre
in an easy-drinking style.

Helderberg Dry Red nv   11
Quinnsworth
Crimson in colour with strawberry jam tones.

Reds between £4.50 and £5.25

Firgrove Pinotage nv 13
(Barry & Fitzwilliam) *Widely available*
Rich with plummy aromas and flavours backed up with
modest tannins.

Helderberg Cabernet Sauvignon 92 12
Quinnsworth
Deep dense plummy fruits with flavour that attacks and
continues right through to the last swallow. Easy-
drinking style.

Helderberg Cabernet Sauvignon/Merlot 94 14
Quinnsworth
Fruit is concentrated and packed with lingering flavour.
Quite a classic finish.

Helderberg Pinotage 94 13
Quinnsworth
Earthy style with lots of dense jammy fruits and austere
finish. Good food wine.

Helderberg Shiraz 94 13
Quinnsworth
Deep minty spicy tones with a good soft centre of fruit
and drying tannins on a long finish.

Kathenberg Cape Red 92 11
(Greenhills) *Widely available*
Easy-drinking with lots of fruit and some length to
finish.

★ **Kathenberg Pinotage 91** 15
(Greenhills) *Widely available*
Solid and gutsy. Plummy-type fruits with a bite of
drying tannin on the finish.

KWV Roodeberg 92 13
(Fitzgeralds) *Wine merchants/off licences*
Blended from several red grape varieties. Ruby in colour
with bags of fruit, supple tannins and a soft lingering
finish.

Van Riebeeck Cabernet Sauvignon 93 12
(Fitzgeralds) *Widely available*
Soft-centred with good fruity appeal.

Van Riebeeck Pinotage 92 13
(Fitzgeralds) *Widely available*
Good colour and easy drinking—a good choice for
everyday drinking.

Reds between £5.25 and £6.50

Culemborg Pinotage 94 12
Dunnes Stores
Bitter-sweet fruits fan out on the palate in a jammy style.
Weighty tannins and good acidity. Easy drinking—a
good choice for a party.

Hippo Creek Merlot/Shiraz 92 13
(Allied Drinks) *Widely available*
These two grapes complement each other in fruit and
structure. Easy drinking in an opulent style.

Hippo Creek Pinotage 93 13
(Allied Drinks) *Widely available*
Deep purple in colour, plum and cherry jam flavours. A
nice bite of acidity and drying tannin add structure.

KWV Cabernet Sauvignon 92 14
(Fitzgeralds) *Wine merchants/off licences*
Lots of cassis fruit aromas that carry right through to the
finish. Balanced acidity and alcohol with some oak
influence.

KWV Cabernet Sauvignon/Shiraz 92   12
(Fitzgeralds)   *Wine merchants/off licences*
An interesting 50/50 blend aged in oak for up to 18
months. Good fruit/vanilla tones in an approachable
style.

KWV Pinotage 92   13
(Fitzgeralds)   *Wine merchants/off licences*
Juicy and fruity with enough tannin and acidity to give
a bite to the finish.

KWV Shiraz 89   14
(Fitzgeralds)   *Wine merchants/off licences*
Quite closed on aroma. Good attack of sweet ripe fruits
which fan out on the palate. Ripe finish with the characteristic Shiraz spice.

Nederburg Cabernet Sauvignon 91   13
(Dillons)   *Widely available*
Lots of plump fruit aromas which deliver on taste. Good
concentration with a supple finish.

Nederburg Pinotage 92   12
(Dillons)   *Widely available*
Sturdy wine with hints of tar on the nose. High acidity
and fruit concentration with drying tannins and some
length on the finish.

Simonsig Pinotage 92   13
(United Beverages)   *Widely available*
Easy-drinking red berry fruit flavours. Good length to
the finish.

Reds between £6.50 and £8

Allesverloren Tinta Barocca 89   13
(Febvre)   *Widely available*
Almost a sweet fruit impact which expands and develops
on the palate. Backed up with drying tannins to give a
long flavoursome finish in the classic claret style.

Bellingham Pinotage 93   14

Dunnes Stores

Satisfying drink with jam-like fruits and a bite of tannin.

Bovlei Pinotage 92   13

(Mitchells)   *Wine merchants/off licences*

Typical jammy fruit aromas and flavours with hints of
cinnamon. Big attack of ripe fruits followed by good
acidity and drying tannins.

Drostdy-Hof Pinotage 93   13

(Febvre)   *Wine merchants/off licences*

The jammy-type fruits that one expects overlain with
drying tannins and a slightly austere finish.

★ **Fleur du Cap Merlot 92**   15

(Febvre)   *Widely available*

Fabulous quality. Dense in colour with plenty of fruit
and velvet suppleness. Only beginning to open up.

Hippo Creek Cabernet Sauvignon 92   13

(Allied Drinks)   *Widely available*

Overlain with vanilla tones. Soft jammy centre with
good length on the finish.

Two Oceans Cabernet Sauvignon/Merlot 95   14

(Febvre)   *Widely available*

Back to the herbs in this deeply coloured wine. Flavours
expand on the palate and end in a long finish.

Villiera Estate Cabernet Sauvignon 90/91   13

(Grants)   *Widely available*

Lots of fruit backed up with structure due to presence of
supple tannins and balanced acidity.

Reds between £8 and £10

Cardouw Pinotage 92   13
(Woodford Bourne)   *Widely available*
Jammy aromas and flavours, firm structure and moderate
tannins.

Fleur du Cap Cabernet Sauvignon 88   14
(Febvre)   *Wine merchants/off licences*
The stamp of classic winemaking. Smoky aroma, new
oak with concentrated flavours of cassis and coffee.

Reds between £10 and £12

Hamilton Russell Pinot Noir 92   14
(Gilbeys)   *Widely available*
A good example of ripe Pinot Noir fruit which develops
on the palate and is supported by mature tannins. Rich,
complex finish.

★ **Meerlust Estate Rubicon 91**   15
(Febvre)   *Wine merchants/off licences*
A classic Bordeaux-style blend of Cabernet Sauvignon,
Cabernet Franc and Merlot. Full-bodied, complex and
concentrated. Great ageing ability. Well worth seeking
out.

OF
RANELAGH
Winner of the
Off-Licence of the Year Award

**Specialists for Wine & Cheese, Spirits, Beers and
Liqueurs**

TEL 497 1739, 496 0552

[219]

Spain

Spain is often called the 'land of contrasts', and any visitor fortunate enough to visit this delightful country extensively would be understandably surprised by the tremendous variations that exist in culture, climate and geographical conditions throughout the various regions. A large country of some 194,000 square miles, it occupies approximately five-sixths of the Iberian Peninsula. It is exceptionally mountainous, with a vast central plateau, and the climate is influenced by both the Atlantic and the Mediterranean. The south has scant rainfall, mild winters and sun-baked summers; the arid central plateau bitterly cold winters and scorching hot summers; while the north enjoys coldish winters, warm summers and considerable rainfall. No wonder there are so many different styles of wine produced from Spain's 1.6 million hectares of vineyards, which account for about 16 per cent of the world's total production of wine.

Wine has been part of Spanish culture for over 3,000 years, since first the Phoenicians and then the Greeks introduced the vine when they settled along the Mediterranean coastline. However, it was the Romans, during their occupation of Spain about 2,000 years ago, who actively encouraged the extensive cultivation of the vine and introduced winemaking techniques that set the standards of quality for centuries to come.

Unfortunately, during the first half of the twentieth century most Spanish winemakers failed to maintain this ancient heritage and, apart from the fine sherries from Andalucia and excellent wines from Rioja, Spain became known as a source of bulk robust wines that were inexpensive, but with little pretension to quality.

Those days have gone, and huge financial investment during the past twenty to thirty years on modern wineries with stainless steel vats and cold fermentation equipment, replanting of many vineyards with better-quality vines and the advent of young innovative winemakers have ensured that Spain can take its place alongside the countries producing the finest of wines.

With a programme of exciting developments within the Spanish wine industry, the future of this 'land of contrasts' as a source of distinctive, high-quality wines looks very bright indeed.

Grape varieties: It is impossible to list all the indigenous grapes of Spain, which number around 600. Many are known by different names in different regions, e.g. Tempranillo is also called Cencibel, Ull de Llebre, Tinto Fino, Tinta de Toro, etc. However, typical examples are:

Black grapes: Tempranillo, Bobal, Garnacha Tinta, Graciano, Cariñena.

White grapes: Airén, Garnacha Blanca, Macabeo, Malvasia, Mersequera, Parellada, Palomino, Pedro Ximenez, Torrontes, Verdejo, Viura (Macabeo), Xarel-lo.

Foreign grapes permitted by some DOs include: (white) Chardonnay, Riesling, Gewürztraminer, Sauvignon Blanc; (red) Cabernet Sauvignon, Malbec, Merlot, Pinot Noir.

Producers: About 1,000 co-operatives throughout the country, responsible for approximately 60% of total production. Remainder controlled by private wineries (*bodegas*).

Quality status: Forty-three wine regions have been granted the Denominación de Origen (DO), equivalent to the French Appellation d'Origine Contrôlée, the first being granted to Rioja in 1926. Rioja is so far the only region to be elevated to a special quality category—Denominacien de Origen Calificada (DOCa), introduced in 1991. Each DO is controlled by a government regulatory body called Consejo Regulador, which monitors all aspects of production. All DOs have their individual seal of authenticity which appears on either the front or back label, along with other relevant information about the quality category and the name of the bottler.

Major DO areas available in Ireland:

Cariñena DO (Aragon) red, white: High-alcohol reds, purple ruby colour with violet aroma. The best are aged for two years. Reasonably good white wines also produced.

Somontano DO (Aragon) (red): Pleasant, easy drinking, light-styled red wines.

Alello DO (red, white, rosé): Small area producing fresh dry white wines, plus a small quantity of red and rosé.

Penedés DO (Catalonia) (red, white, rosé, sparkling): Excellent dry white wines and the majority of Cava (sparkling) from this region. Also first-class red wines, some with ageing potential.

Priorato DO (Catalonia) (red, white): Small mountainous area making very good full-bodied red wines of high alcohol content. Some whites produced—most famous is a speciality 'Rancio'—oxidised and dry, medium or sweet.

Costers Del Segre DO (red, white, rosé, sparkling): Impressive red, white, rosé and sparkling wines from the famous Raimat estate.

Ribeiro DO (Galacia) (red, white, rosé): Good dry white wine ideal with local seafood, plus some sound reds.

Navarra DO (Navarra) (red, white, rosé): This region produces high-quality reserva red wines, similar to neighbouring Rioja. Also large production of basic reds, fruity rosé and white wines.

La Mancha DO (New Castile) (red, white): Huge area producing about 35% of Spain's total wine. Mostly white, from the Airén grape, and a considerable improvement in quality during recent years.

Valdepenas DO (New Castile) (red, white): A southerly enclave of La Mancha, producing good light reds, and a few bodegas age reds in oak for reservas. Average quality wines, but improving.

Ribera Del Duero DO (Old Castile) (red, rosé): Mostly red wines plus some rosé. The reds are elegant and need time to develop. The best, and most expensive in Spain, is 'Vega Sicilia'.

Rueda DO (Old Castile) (white): Very good quality dry white wines. Some bodegas using foreign grapes, e.g. Sauvignon Blanc.

Toro DO (Old Castile) (red): Robust high-alcohol red wines which have shown a marked improvement in quality during the past few years. The best age well.

Rioja DOCa (Rioja) (red, white, rosé): The best-known red wines of Spain which are classified according to quality and length of ageing. The finest are Gran Reservas and Reservas, but some excellent reds are now made without the traditional ageing in oak and bottle. Most whites are clean and dry, but tend to be unexciting.

Valencia DO (Valencia) (red, white): Large areas of production with more white than red. Very Mediterranean in style, with high alcohol and low acidity; usually big wines. Quality has improved in recent years. Other DOs in this region include Yecla and Utiel-Requena.

Tom Franks

WHITE WINES

Whites under £4.50

Campo Verde Cariñena DO nv   13
(Greenhills)   *Widely available*
Easy-drinking with a bite of acidity.

Marqués de Bajamar Navarra DO 94   13
Dunnes Stores
Stewed apple aromas with a fresh appealing taste due to crisp acidity.

Senorio de Urdaix Navarra DO 94   13
(Reynolds)   *Widely available*
Pale with crisp fruit flavours and refreshing acidity.

Albor Campo Viejo Rioja DOCa 93   11
(Cassidy)   *Widely available*

Easy-drinking, medium acidity and quite a short finish.

Don Darias Vino de Mesa nv   11
(Barry & Fitzwilliam)   *Widely available*
Oxidative style with fat, almost herbal tones.

Faustino Rivero Ylecia Rioja DOCa 93   12
(Barry & Fitzwilliam)   *Widely available*
Fat yeasty traditional style, at its best served very cool.

Gandia Chardonnay Utiel-Requeña DO nv   11
(Barry & Fitzwilliam)   *Widely available*
A dry white wine short on the finish but clean and well
made.

Jaume Serra Macabeo Penedès DO 94   12
(Mackenway)   *Widely available*
Surprisingly fresh and crisp. Very pleasant with good
acidity and fruit tones.

Roblejano nv   11
(Gilbeys)   *Widely available*
A broad style of wine—rich fruit overlain with a hint of
toffee.

Viña Hermosa Rioja DOCa 94   13
(Reynolds)   *Widely available*
Straightforward juicy fruity style with easy appeal.

Whites between £5.25 and £6.50

Can Feixes Blanc Seleccio Penedès DO 94   13
(Reynolds)   *Widely available*
Produced from the Parellada, Macabeo and Chardonnay
grapes. This wine has easy drinking appeal.

Faustino VII Rioja DOCa 93   12
(Gilbeys)   *Widely available*
Hints of ripe melon cut through with citrus acidity and
good length of flavour.

[225]

Royal Soledad Rioja DOCa 93   11
(Jenkinson)   *Wine merchants/off licences*
Lemon tinged with hints of grapefruit on the palate.
Crisp citrus-type acidity and some length to finish.

Torres Vina Sol Penedès DO 94   14
(Woodford Bourne)   *Widely available*
Pale in colour with tinges of green. Fresh, clean apple-
type fruits with crisp acidity.

Viñas del Vero Chenin Blanc Somontano DO 94   11
(Mackenway)   *Widely available*
Don't be put off by the aroma—much better on the
palate with soft ripe fruits in a broad style.

Whites between £6.50 and £8

Marqués de Alella Classico Penedès DO 93   13
(Jenkinson)   *Wine merchants/off licences*
Light, off-dry style with good lemon-type acidity in an
easy-drinking style.

Marqués de Griñon Durius Toledo DO 93   13
(Fitzgeralds)   *Wine merchants/off licences*
For the ABC drinker (anything but Chardonnay). Ignore
the aroma as it is far better on the palate. Stewed apples
with a squeeze of lemon juice acidity.

Montecillo Vina Cumbrero Rioja DOCa 93   12
(Dillons)   *Widely available*
Easy-drinking Rioja delivers on fruit and finishes
smoothly.

Torres Gran Vina Sol Chardonnay Penedès DO 93   14
(Woodford Bourne)   *Widely available*
Pleasant floral aromas open out on the palate, ending in
a spicy finish.

**Viñas del Vero Barrel Fermented Chardonnay
Somontano DO 93**   13

(Mackenway)   *Widely available*
Spicy new oak influence with good balancing acidity
and alcohol. The pleasant toasty finish adds interest.

Viñas del Vero Gewürztraminer Somontano DO 94   13
(Mackenway)   *Widely available*
Characteristic Turkish Delight aromas that carry
through on flavour and end in a spicy finish.

> Whites between £8 and £10

★ **Marqués de Murrieta Rioja Reserva DOCa 91**   15
(Gilbeys)   *Widely available*
An all-time favourite. Big and opulent with a rich
luscious finish and a smack of fruit on the end.

Viña Ardanza Rioja Reserva La Rioja Alta DOCa 89   14
(Woodford Bourne)   *Wine merchants/off licences*
Pungent style with lemon-type acidity and some length
on the finish.

> White between £10 and £12

Torres Fransola Penedès DO 93   13
(Woodford Bourne)   *Wine merchants/off licences*
Oak-aged Sauvignon Blanc. Attractive herbaceous scents
with creamy tones on the palate and a long fruity finish.

RED WINES

> Reds under £4.50

Campo Rojo nv   13
(Greenhills)   *Widely available*
Easy-drinking at a good price. Deep in colour with lots
of plummy flavour.

★ **Fuente del Ritmo Tempranillo La Mancha DO 93**   15
                                               Quinnsworth
What a bargain! Chocolate, ripe blackcurrants and toast,
with an extra long finish. Great value for money.

Marqués de Bajamar Navarra DO 94   13
Dunnes Stores

Ruby in colour with jammy fruit flavours. Drink young and cool.

Senorio de Urdaix Navarra DOC 94   13
(Reynolds)   *Widely available*

Soft and appealing with sweet ripe fruit attack and supple texture.

Vina Albali Reserva Valdepenas DO 87   14
Superquinn

Soft supple easy drinking with strawberry fruit tones and a nice smack of vanilla. Great party wine.

Reds between £4.50 and £5.25

Albor Campo Viejo Rioja DOCa 94   12
(Cassidy)   *Widely available*

New style Rioja made for early drinking. Smooth fruity style with instant appeal.

Allozo Tempranillo La Mancha DO 91   12
Quinnsworth

Dense and fruity with liquorice overtones. Hint of plummy fruit on the palate with drying tannins on the finish.

Almenar Rioja Crianza DOCa 92   13
Dunnes Stores

Earthy dusty aromas followed by a soft jammy flavour. Easy drinking style.

Berberana Tempranillo Rioja DOCa 93   13
Quinnsworth

Refreshing. Light ruby in colour with fig-like fruit tones and a soft easy finish.

Cermeño Toro DO 92   13
(Reynolds)   *Widely available*

Deep in colour. Big, bold and meaty.

Conde Bel Rioja DOCa 93   12
(Jenkinson)   *Wine merchants/off licences*
Purple toned with hints of red berry fruits. Pleasant
spicy finish with a hint of drying tannin.

Don Darias nv   12
(Barry & Fitzwilliam)   *Widely available*
Silky texture and easy drinkability.

Faustino Rivero Ylecia Rioja DOCa 94   12
(Barry & Fitzwilliam)   *Widely available*
Lush and chewy with plenty of jammy fruit.

Gandia Cabernet Sauvignon Utiel-Requeña DO nv   12
(Barry & Fitzwilliam)   *Widely available*
Wine-gums and raspberry jelly. Easy-drinking.

Gandia Tempranillo Utiel-Requeña DO nv   12
(Barry & Fitzwilliam)   *Widely available*
Ageing in oak adds a dimension to this easy-drinking
wine. Strawberry fruit aromas.

Jaume Serra Tempranillo Penedès DO 93   12
(Mackenway)   *Widely available*
Rioja style with creamy fruits, coconut aromas and
harmonious tannins.

★ **Marqués d'Aragon Garnacha Puro Calatayud DO 94**   15
Searsons
Marvellous concentration of herbs and fruit. Think of
cold tea and ripe plums ending in a long super rich
finish.

Castillo del Ebro Navarra DO 93   13
(Mitchells)   *Wine merchants/off licences*
Opaque in colour. Perfume on the nose reminiscent of
violets. Integrated tannins with a very pleasant lingering
finish.

Roblejano nv   12
(Gilbeys)   *Widely available*
Spicy and jammy in an easy to drink style. Good party
wine.

Valdeoliva Toro DO 92   14
(Reynolds)   *Widely available*
Deep crimson in colour with hints of tobacco and firm
tannins ending in a flavoursome finish.

Vina Hermosa Rioja DOCa 94   13
(Reynolds)
Garnacha and Tempranillo grape varieties give an
appealing youthful fragrance of berry fruits which
deliver on flavour.

Reds between £5.25 and £6.50

Colegiata Toro DO 91   13
(Mackenway)   *Wine merchants/off licences*
Another good example of the styles emerging from
Spain. Lots of stewed fruits mingled with spice and
ending in an earthy tone. Needs more time to show its
promise.

Dama de Toro DO 92   13
(Mackenway)   *Wine merchants/off licences*
Powerful aromas of meaty extract. On the palate, has
intense damson-type fruits with drying tannins and high
alcohol. Good food wine.

Faustino VII Rioja DOCa 91   13
(Gilbeys)   *Widely available*
Squashed strawberry fruits overlain with coconut/
vanilla tones, ending in a lingering supple finish.

Marqués de Griñon Durius Toledo DO 93   13
(Fitzgeralds)   *Wine merchants/off licences*
Depth of colour and warm ripe blackberry fruits
overlain with mint, held together with chewy tannins.

Marqués de Griñon Rioja DOCa 92   14
(Fitzgeralds)   *Wine merchants/off licences*
Purple-toned, lots of cherry-like fruits. Very well
balanced with supple tannins and good use of oak.

Royal Rioja DOCa 93   13
(Jenkinson)   *Wine merchants/off licences*
Easy-drinking, smooth supple wine with hints of spice
and pleasant oak tones.

Torres Coronas Penedès DO 91   14
(Woodford Bourne)   *Widely available*
Deep in colour with pleasant blackberry-type fruits
carrying through on flavour and ending in a smooth
finish.

Torres Sangre de Toro Penedès DO 92   13
(Woodford Bourne)   *Widely available*
Lots of jammy fruit appeal which carries through on
flavour.

Viña Hermosa Rioja Crianza Rioja DOCa 92   14
(Reynolds)   *Widely available*
Good strawberry fruit and medium length on the finish.

Reds between £6.50 and £8

Berberana Rioja Reserva DOCa 88   14
Quinnsworth
Tile brick in colour. Drinking well now with attractive
tobacco and cedar overtones. Lots of tannin but fruit
fights back, ending in a kick of spice.

Campo Viejo Rioja Reserva DOCa 89   14
(Cassidy)   *Widely available*
Advanced maturity. Very pleasant, dominated by plum
and coconut aromas. Supple and silky with oaky tones
that linger.

Canusverus Crianza Toro DO 89
(Reynolds)   14
                                     Widely available
An assertive wine, big meaty overtones and intense long
finish.

Cune Rioja Crianza DOCa 91
(Findlaters)   12
                                     Widely available
Soft fruity tones with an elegant medium long finish.

Colegiata Reserva Toro DO 89
(Mackenway)   14
                        Wine merchants/off licences
Aged in American oak. Chunky fruit aromas and
flavours. The tannins have rounded to give suppleness,
and an added touch of maturity and complexity.

Guelbenzu Navarra DOC 90
                                              14
                                          Searsons
Full fruity nose, dense colour and long tea-like finish.

★Marqués de Cáceres Rioja DOCa 91
(Grants)   15
                                     Widely available
Firm in structure with lots of savoury meaty extract and
the hallmark of oak. Stands out from the crowd.

Montecillo Vina Cumbrero Rioja DOCa 89
(Dillons)   13
                                     Widely available
Squashed strawberries and hints of vanilla add up to
pleasant drinking.

★Olarra Rioja Crianza DOCa 91
(Allied Drinks)   15
                                     Widely available
Super rich aromas and flavours of ripe red berry fruits
with lots of vanilla tones.

Siglo Rioja DOCa 92
(Mitchells)   13
                                     Widely available
Note the sacking covering the bottle. Tile brick in colour,
pleasant coconut aromas in a style of Rioja that is not
over-oaked.

Solana Ribero DO 14
(Cassidy) *Widely available*
Inky in colour with all the richness of Tempranillo.
Modern style Spanish.

★ **Taja Jumilla DO 92** 15
Searsons

Rich and savoury with liquorice and lots of fruity
extract, drying tannin and a long rich finish. Oozes
appeal.

Torres Gran Sangre de Toro Reserva Penedès DO 89 14
(Woodford Bourne) *Widely available*
Lots of soft ripe fruit tones and oak influence, fine
lingering finish.

**Viñas del Vero Tempranillo/Cabernet Sauvignon
Somantano DO 91** 13
(Mackenway) *Wine merchants/off licences*
The combination of Tempranillo and Cabernet
Sauvignon with oak influence adds up to delicious
supple drinking with a long lingering finish.

Reds between £8 and £10

Alberdi Rioja DOCa 89 13
(Woodford Bourne) *Widely available*
Complex nose of tobacco and spice in a classic style.

Can Feixes Negre Seleccio Penedès DO 91 14
(Reynolds) *Wine merchants/off licences*
Ull de Llebre (Tempranillo) delivers on soft fruity
aromas and flavours ending in a lush finish.

★ **Conde de Valdemar Rioja Reserva DOCa 90** 15
(Febvre) *Widely available*
Big in structure and big in flavour. Excellent balance
with a lingering lush finish.

★**Marqués de Riscal Rioja Reserva DOCa 90**   15
(Findlaters)   *Widely available*
Rich, opulent and oaky. Has all the hallmarks of classic
Rioja with the fruit dominated by a hint of coconut.

Viña Hermosa Rioja Gran Reserva DOCa 85   13
(Reynolds)   *Widely available*
Generous and ripe for drinking now with its firm
structure and vanilla overtones.

**Viñas del Vero Merlot/Cabernet Sauvignon Reserva
Somontano DO 91**   14
(Mackenway)   *Wine merchants/off licences*
Another stunning example of good wine making.
Loaded with fruit cake aromas and flavours. Easy
supple drinking.

Reds between £10 and £12

Bodegas Olarra Anares Rioja Gran Reserva DOCa 87
14
(Allied Drinks)   *Widely available*
Smooth texture and fruity overtones, with that wonderful
vanilla tone.

Bordon Rioja Gran Reserva DOCa 82   13
(Jenkinson)   *Wine merchants/off licences*
Oaky vanilla flavour with ripe strawberry fruits and a
smooth texture.

★★**Faustino I Rioja Gran Reserva DOCa 87**   16
(Gilbeys)   *Widely available*
A deliciously opulent wine, with sweet strawberry and
banana fruits, vanilla influence and a silky texture.

★**Marqués de Murrieta Rioja Reserva DOCa 91**   15
(Gilbeys)   *Widely available*
A great favourite. Big and opulent with a rich luscious
finish and smack of fruit on the end.

Red between £12 and £15

★ **Cune Imperial Rioja Reserva DOCa 88**   15
(Findlaters)   *Wine merchants/off licences*
Smooth silky Rioja with a big mouthfilling finish of oak
and red fruits.

Reds between £20 and £30

Montecillo Vina Monty Rioja Gran Reserva DOCa 85   14
(Dillons)   *Wine merchants/off licences*
Rioja at this age assumes a bouquet of complex cedar
tones.The oak and spice are all there with ripe fruits
cutting through.

★ **Torres Gran Coronas Mas la Plana Gran Reserva
Penedès DO 88**   17
(Woodford Bourne)   *Wine merchants/off licences*
A fabulous wine richly concentrated with liquorice
tones overlain with spicy oak and blackberry fruits.
Long flavoursome finish.

ROSÉ WINE

Rosé between £6.50 and £8

Marqués de Riscal Rosado Rioja DOCa   13
(Findlaters)   *Widely available*
Squashed berry fruits. Quite broad in flavour with quite
a refreshing finish.

Champagne and Sparkling Wines

Champagne—the very word conjures up thoughts of celebration, excitement, success, weddings, and just what have racing drivers got against it? Champagne is the greatest of all sparkling wines and the skill of making it was invented and perfected in the region of the same name in northern France. It is the unique combination of soil, grape varieties and winemaking that produces wines of great finesse and individual flavour.

Sparkling wine contains bubbles of carbon dioxide; they are the result of a second fermentation which takes place either in the bottle or in a vat. In the traditional or Champagne method this second fermentation takes place in the bottle and is the result of a long and labour-intensive process that starts in the vineyard and continues in the cellar until the wine is ready for release. A less expensive method is called *cuve close* or closed tank, where the second fermentation takes place in a sealed tank. The wine is then filtered under pressure and bottled.

Apart from Champagne there are a number of other regions in France that produce sparkling wine, including the Loire with sparkling Saumur and Crémant de Loire, Alsace with Crémant d'Alsace and the Midi with Blanquette de Limoux.

Spain is a major producer of sparkling wine, called Cava, which is made by the traditional method. Most Cava comes from the Penedés region of northern Spain.

The Italians love sparkling wine and Italy produces a wide range, from wines with just a gentle sparkle to fully sparkling, spumante wines. Asti Spumante is the best known, made with the Muscat grape which gives its pungent fruitiness to the wine.

Germany produces a large amount of sparkling wine called Sekt, most of it made by the tank method. The Germans drink most of this Sekt themselves; per capita consumption of sparkling wine in Germany is the highest in the world.

Sparkling wine from the New World comes primarily from California and Australia as well as New Zealand and even Brazil. The wines are made by both traditional and tank methods and represent good value for money.

Champagne region

Champagne is produced only in the Champagne region of northern France, about 80 miles north-east of Paris. Within the EU only sparkling wine produced in the Champagne region of France may bear the name of Champagne.

Vineyard areas

The three main vineyard areas are Vallée de la Marne, Montagne de Reims and Côte des Blancs. The main centres where most of the Champagne houses have their offices and cellars are the cathedral city of Reims and the town of Epernay.

Climate and soil

The Champagne vineyards are the most northerly vineyards in France and the climate is such that the grapes just about ripen, producing a light crisp wine which is ideal as a base for making sparkling wine. The soil is mainly chalk, covered by a thin layer of topsoil.

Grape varieties

Three main grape varieties are used in the making of Champagne, two black grapes, Pinot Noir and Pinot Meunier, and one white, Chardonnay. Most Champagne is made from a blend of these three varieties.

Styles

Non-vintage (nv): The most popular style of Champagne, this is a *cuvée* or blend of wines of more than one year, representing the style of the producing house. *Vintage:* The best-quality wine of a single year, more full-bodied and with the potential to improve for a number of years. *Rosé:* Pink Champagne or rosé is usually made by blending in a little red wine. *Cuvée de Prestige:* Most houses produce a prestige wine made from the highest-quality base wines blended with great care.

Producers

Though some growers make and sell their own Champagne, most sell their grapes to one of the large Champagne houses, which produce the most famous brands, or to a co-operative.

Labels

Champagne is a protected name and must appear on the label and the cork of every bottle. Within the EU only sparkling wine produced in the Champagne region of France may bear the name of Champagne. The label will also give the maker's name and address (Reims, Épernay, Ay) and, if a vintage, the vintage date. There will also be a term indicating the style of the wine. *Brut*, the most popular style, means dry to very dry. *Extra dry* is in fact a little sweeter than Brut and *Demi-sec* is sweet.

David Power

CHAMPAGNE

Between £15 and £20	

Mumm Cordon Rouge Brut nv 12
(Barry & Fitzwilliam) *Widely available*
Ripe fruit tones make this less dry. Good flavour
development and some length to finish.

Between £20 and £30	

Billecart-Salmon Brut nv 13
(Brangan) *Widely available*
Rich yet subtle fruit flavours, with characteristic biscuity
tones.

★**Bollinger Special Cuvée Brut nv**   15
(Woodford Bourne)   *Widely available*
Stylish champagne—big and bold with concentrated
fruit aromas and flavour, finishing in a pleasant toasty
aftertaste.

Charles Heidsieck Brut Reserve nv   14
(Remy)   *Widely available*
Pleasant creamy biscuit tones follow through on flavour.
Elegant and stylish.

★ **Dravigny Demoizet 1er Cru Selection Brut nv**   15
                                         Burgundy Direct
Delicate fruit with good bubbly mousse and fresh
acidity. Superb quality with a distinct yeasty flavour.

Lanson Black Label nv   12
(Grants)   *Widely available*
Distinctive with delicate fruit flavours and a pungent
yeasty tone which is the hallmark of champagne.

Laurent-Perrier Brut nv   13
(Gilbeys)   *Wine merchants/off licences*
Always consistent in quality with a good persistence of
bubble bead and light fresh apple flavours with a
biscuity background.

Möet et Chandon Brut Imperial 86   13
(Dillons)   *Wine merchants/off licences*
Delivers much more on taste than aroma. Note the fine
bubble with creamy flavours and lively acidity.

Piper Heidsieck Brut nv   13
(Remy)   *Widely available*
Creamy mousse with nice hints of apple-type fruits.
Crisp acidity leaves a clean fresh finish.

Pol Roger Extra Dry nv 14
(Barry & Fitzwilliam) *Widely available*
Appealing yeasty tones and a clean fresh finish.

★ **Roederer Brut Premier nv** 15
(Searsons) *Wine merchants/off licences*
Superbly balanced with lots of ripe citrus and apple fruit
tones. Creamy biscuity finish. Value for money.

Taittinger Brut nv 13
(Gilbeys) *Wine merchants/off licences*
Ripe fruit tones follow through on creamy mousse and
end in a yeasty bread-like finish.

★ **Krug Grande Cuvée nv** 15
(Remy) *Wine merchants/off licences*
Complex and elegant. The intense fruity aromas and
buttery biscuit tones are supported by a fine firm
mousse. Superb quality.

★ **Möet et Chanon Dom Pérignon 85** 15
(Dillons) *Wine merchants/off licences*
Elegant and subtle. Enticing aromas of apples mingling
with biscuit end in a suggestion of toast and nuts.

ROSÉ CHAMPAGNE

Between £30 and £50

Billecart Salmon Brut Rosé nv 13
(Brangan) *Widely available*
An attractive salmon colour. Lively fruit flavours
reminiscent of strawberry and finishing with a pleasant
lively acidity.

★★ **Bollinger Grande Année 85** 16
(Woodford Bourne) *Wine merchants/off licences*
Rich buttery tones with a good attack of lively fruit
which opens, develops and finishes in a cloud of flavour
and bubble. Outstanding.

SPARKLING WINES

Between £8 and £10

Aliança Bairrada Bruto 91 (Portugal) 13
(Reynolds) *Widely available*
Light green-tinged colour with good mousse, fresh
lively acidity and some length to finish.

Freixenet Carta Nevada Semi-Seco nv (Spain) 12
(Woodford Bourne) *Widely available*
Crisp and fresh in style with pleasant mousse and a
touch of nuttiness on the finish. Medium dry finish.

Freixenet Cordon Negro Brut nv (Spain) 14
(Woodford Bourne) *Widely available*
Rich and nutty in style with some yeastiness and a
medium long finish.

Henkell Trocken nv (Germany) 11
(Searsons) *Wine merchants/off licences*
Nice fine mousse with good acidity and fresh fruit.

Lancers Brut nv (Portugal) 12
(Gilbeys) *Widely available*
With its distinctive bottle shape, this is the ultimate
'quaffing' medium sweet wine produced from the
Periquita grape of Portugal.

Medium Dry Blue Nun nv (Germany) 11
(Dillons) *Widely available*
Easy-drinking fruity sparkling wine.

Yalumba Angas Brut nv (Australia) 11
(Findlaters) *Widely available*
After opening, the mousse lasted for several days. Deep
yellow in colour with fruity tones and pleasant mousse.

Between £10 and £12

Asti Spumante Martini & Rossi nv (Italy) 13
(Grants) *Widely available*

Often snubbed by wine drinkers this easy drinking wine is driven by the ripe fruity flavours of the Moscato grape. Lively acidity cuts through the sweet grapey fruit. Try it chilled with strawberries.

Blanquette de Limoux Diaphane Brut 88 (France)   12
Mitchells

Reputed to be France's oldest sparkling wine. Subtle yeasty tones. The addition of Chardonnay to the traditional Mauzac and Chenin grape varieties has added greatly to the overall quality.

Château Moncontour Brut AC Vouvray 92 (France)   13
(Febvre)   *Widely available*

Fine example of stylish sparkling wines. Apple aromas and flavours with good mousse and a crisp finish.

Codorníu Première Cuvée Brut nv (Spain)   12
(Grants)   *Widely available*

Fresh and crisp with elegant mousse and a long subtle fruity finish make this a popular choice. Cava is at its best drunk young and fresh.

Collavini Il Grigio Brut DOC nv (Italy)   14
(Ecock)   *Wine merchants/off licences*

Italy produces very fine quality sparkling wines. Made from 100% Chardonnay, this one has good-quality fruit and great finesse.

Cuvée Napa Mumm Brut nv (California)   13
(Barry & Fitzwilliam)   *Widely available*

Exotic fruit tones with lively mousse and a good clean finish.

Montana Lindauer Brut nv (New Zealand)   13
(Grants)   *Widely available*

Hard to beat for value and style. Subtle fruity tones with lots of bubble and bite.

Between £12 and £15

Caves de Lugney AC Crémant de Bourgogne Brut nv
(France)   12
(Mackenway)   *Wine merchants/off licences*
Produced from 100% Chardonnay, this wine has a nice
creamy mousse with hints of peach. Classic
presentation.

Gratien & Meyer AC Saumur Brut nv (France)   13
(Gilbeys)   *Widely available*
Good mousse which holds up in the glass. A dry finish.
This famous house from the Loire also produces a
pleasant fruity rosé style.

Henri Grandin Brut nv (France)   12
(Febvre)   *Wine merchants/off licences*
A nice bite of apple fruit is cut through with zesty
acidity and followed by a pleasant biscuity aftertaste.

Pongracz Brut nv (South Africa)   13
(Febvre)   *Wine merchants/off licences*
A fair quality/price ratio. Reminiscent of good
champagne. Biscuity flavours, long length on the finish.

Schramsberg Blanc de Blancs Brut 88 (California)   13
                                                    Terroirs
Produced from Chardonnay and Pinot Blanc. Made by
the traditional method. Delicate floral aromas, fine
mousse and a dry yet fruity finish.

Between £15 and £20

Bredif AC Vouvray Brut nv (France)   13
(Gilbeys)   *Wine merchants/off licences*
A nice example of a zesty, well-made sparkling wine
with good apple-type flavours and fine mousse
produced from the Chenin Blanc grape.

Gaston Huet AC Vouvray nv (France)   14
(Brangan)   *Widely available*
Excellent buttery aromas and flavours that linger on the

finish. Worth the extra cost.

Pelorus 89 (New Zealand)   13
(Findlaters)   *Wine merchants/off licences*
From the famous Cloudy Bay winery, this sparkling
wine is quite 'broad' in flavour with a luscious texture
and good depth of flavour.

SPARKLING ROSÉ

Between £8 and £10

Yalumba Angas Brut Rosé nv (Australia)   12
(Findlaters)   *Widely available*
Easy drinking. Lots of bubble and zest, full gooseberry
and apple-type flavours.

Dessert Wines

Whether sipped chilled on their own, or matched with appropriate foods such as fine pâté, blue cheese or fruit-based desserts, the richness of good sweet wines is an experience in itself. Few wines have such an unrivalled variety of taste sensations.

Sauternes, Bordeaux

Sauternes is the name of the wine area and appellation from the Bordeaux region. Sémillon is the dominant grape variety, with some Sauvignon Blanc and Muscadelle. When climatic conditions are right *pourriture noble* (noble rot) develops on the thin-skinned Sémillon grape. The grapes shrivel, concentrating the sugar. The grapes are then individually picked at their maximum sugar concentration.

These wines are expensive and rare, but because of their intensity and complexity a little goes a long way. Note the concentration of rich honeyed aromas and tastes that go on and on. The wine is luscious, yet held in balance by an acidity that allows the complexity to show through. The following examples of Sauternes were tasted and rated highly by the panel:

Château de la Chartreuse 88 (Quinnsworth)
Château la Bouade 92 (Dunnes Stores)

Also highly recommended but not tasted by the panel are the following Premier Crus:

Château Coutet (Barsac) (Searsons)
Château Filhot (Febvre)
Château Lafaurie-Peyraguey (United Beverages)
Château Rieussec (Searsons).

Hungary

Tokaji Aszú (Tokay) is the fabled dessert wine from northern Hungary. Produced from late-picked Aszú grapes affected by noble rot (Botrytis cinerea). The panel tasted and liked *Tokaji 5 Puttonyos Aszú* (Searsons) with its nutty character and good acidity.

Australia

Brown Brothers Orange Muscat and Flora (Woodford Bourne): This wine is called after the two white grape varieties from which it is made. The Orange Muscat is part of the Muscat family of grapes originating in south-east France. Wines made from this grape are always extremely aromatic and words such as marmalade and orange blossom are often used to describe them. Flora is a variety produced from a cross between the Sémillon and Gewürztraminer grapes. The panel commented on its low alcohol, golden glints, intense marmalade aromas and long finish.

Carlyle Estate Liqueur Muscat: Produced from the Muscat Blanc à Petits Grains (brown Muscat), semi-raisined grapes are partially fermented and fortified with grape spirit. They are then subject to long cask ageing. Burnt toffee in colour and aroma. High alcohol packs a punch and the sweet caramel soft tone should appeal to those who like 'sticky' drinks.

D'Arenberg McLaren Vale Noble Riesling (Taserra): This dessert wine is produced from Riesling grapes in an advanced state of Botrytis cinerea. Deep golden with amber glints. Rich and ripe with raisiny botrytised honey appeal. Excellent limey acidity cuts straight through the luscious fruit.

Fortified Wines

Many people, even in the wine trade, are confused by the terms 'fortified wines' and 'liqueur wines', particularly since there has been a change of definition within the EU, but really it is quite simple. There are light wines, sometimes called table wines by the English-speaking trade, which are made in the ordinary, traditional way by fermenting grape juice. If, during the fermentation process, all the sugar is not converted into alcohol and CO_2 a naturally sweet wine is the result. Then there are fortified wines to which alcohol is added during or after fermentation has taken place and the wine has been made.

The most important of the fortified wines are Port and Sherry, which are completely different in character. One difference is that Sherry is fermented dry, in other words all the sugar is turned into alcohol and the level of sweetness is adjusted later. All Sherry starts out as dry wine; the high alcohol content is achieved by fortifying the wine with grape spirit. The range of styles is due to this process of fortification and the maturation of the wine. When making Port, however, fermentation is stopped at a very early stage by adding grape spirit, so that a considerable amount of sweetness is retained in the finished wine, which is high in alcohol. In colour Port can be red, tawny or white.

One of the comments frequently made about these two great fortified wines is that they are drinks made by foreigners for foreigners. There is a certain historical truth in this statement, since in the late eighteenth and early nineteenth centuries it was only Spaniards living near Jerez and the western part of Andalucia who drank Sherry. It was hard to find even in other parts of Spain. This applies less to Port, because one could nearly always find vintage Port throughout Portugal, but the export trade, as such, developed very much in the nineteenth century.

Fortified wines also include a number of high-strength wines produced in the South of France and in Italy, such as the Vins Doux Naturels. These wines are produced in a similar way to Port in that they also have their fermentation stopped by the addition of grape spirit in order to retain natural sweetness while increasing the alcohol content.

The other great fortified wine is, of course, Marsala, which is a rich dessert wine to which alcohol is added. It is produced in Sicily.

George O'Malley

STYLES OF SHERRY

Fino

Produced in Jerez and Puerto de Santa María, Fino is matured under a layer of flor yeast which helps preserve freshness and avoids oxidation. Very pale in colour; bone dry, elegant with a pungent delicate bouquet of almonds. Leaves the palate whistle clean. Good examples include:

Croft Delicado (Gilbeys)
Domecq La Ina (Fitzgeralds)
Gonzalez Byass Elegante (Gilbeys)
Gonzales Byass Tio Pepe (Gilbeys)
Osborne Pale Dry (Barry & Fitzwilliam)
Pando (Woodford Bourne)
River Fly (Findlaters)
Sandeman Seco (Dillons)
University Fino (Mitchells)

Manzanilla

A very dry Fino from the town of Sanlúcar de Barrameda. Very pale with characteristic pungency and nutty tones with a slight salty edge to the finish. Good examples include:

Almacenista Manzanilla, Lustau (Mitchells)
Osborne (Barry & Fitzwilliam)
Papirusa, Lustau (Mitchells)—this one is superb, delicate and very dry

Amontillado

Indicates a style which has lost 'flor' yeast. Light amber in colour with hazelnut/walnut aromas. Dry or medium dry. Good examples include:
Caballero (Gilbeys)
Croft Classic (Gilbeys)
Domecq Double Century (Fitzgeralds)
Dry Fly (Findlaters)
Gonzalez Byass La Concha (Gilbeys)
Harveys Club (Grants)
Sandeman Medium Dry (Dillons)
University Amontillado (Mitchells)
Williams & Humbert Dry Sack (Woodford Bourne)

Palo Cortado

A type of wine that falls between the styles of Fino, Amontillado and Oloroso. Always well balanced with a rich caramel tone combined with roasted nuts. Dark amber in colour. This is a rare and interesting style of Sherry. Highly prized, it is worth the extra cost. Good examples available in Ireland include:
Peninsula, Lustau (Mitchells)
Williams & Humbert Dos Cortades (Woodford Bourne)

Oloroso

A style of Sherry that never developed flor and has been fortified up to 18°. In colour ranging from dark gold to rich amber; can be dry or sweet with a nutty, raisiny flavour.

Dry Oloroso

Deep amber with rich full caramel and cooked raisin flavours. A good example is:
Almacenista Oloroso, Lustau (Mitchells)

Cream Oloroso

Deep brown with rich fruity aromas and deep caramel flavours in a sweet style. Good examples include:
Lake Fly Sweet (Findlaters)

[249]

Osborne Medium (Barry & Fitzwilliam)
Sandeman (Dillons)
Walnut Brown (Woodford Bourne)
Williams & Humbert A Winter's Tale (Woodford Bourne)

Pale Cream

Fino-based, pale in colour, rich, sweet and creamy with intense dried fruit flavours. Good examples include:
Croft Original (Gilbeys)
Domecq Double Century (Fitzgeralds)
Harveys Bristol Cream (Grants)
Osborne Cream (Barry & Fitzwilliam)
University Cream (Mitchells)
University Pale (Mitchells)
Williams & Humbert Canasta Cream (Woodford Bourne)
Williams & Humbert Dry Sack (Woodford Bourne)

STYLES OF PORT

Vintage Port

Only declared in certain years of outstanding quality. The wines do most of their maturing in bottle for up to twenty years, so they throw a heavy sediment in the bottle and have to be decanted. Noted for their deep crimson colour, smooth velvety texture and rich peppery finish. Generally declared vintages include: 91, 85, 83, 82, 80, 77, 75, 70, 66, 63. Vintage Port is not produced every year. Not every House declares a vintage in the same year.
Cálem 77 (Cassidy)
Churchill 85, 91 (Findlaters)
Cockburns 83 (Grants)
Croft 85 (Gilbeys)
Dow's 77, 80, 83, 85, 91 (James Adams)
Dow's 63, 66, 70, 77, 83 (Karwig)
Ferreira 77 (Reynolds)
Fonseca 80, 85 (Mitchells)
Fonseca-Guimaraens 76, 78 (Mitchells)
Graham's Malvedos 79, 84 (Fitzgeralds)

Graham's Vintage 80, 83, 85 (Fitzgeralds)
Offley 83, 85, 87 (Allied Drinks)
Offley's Boa Vista 77 (Searsons)
Osborne 70 (Barry & Fitzwilliam)
Pitters 53 (bottled 88) (Tassera)
Pocas 82 (Cassidy)
Sandemans 82, 85 (Dillons)
Taylor's 77, 83, 85 (Woodford Bourne)
Taylor's 70 (Searsons)
Warre's 75 (Grants)

Late Bottled Vintage (LBV)

A Port of a single year which has been matured in cask and bottled in its fourth to sixth year. The wine has already thrown its sediment in cask and does not require decanting. Full flavoured with velvet-like texture and smooth raisin fruit with a little tartness on the end.
Cockburn's Anno 88, 89 (Grants)
Croft 87 (Gilbeys)
Graham's 88 (Fitzgerald)
Offley 85 (Allied Drinks)
Porto Noval 88 (Barry & Fitzwilliam)
Sandeman 87, 89 (Dillons)
Taylor's 89 (Woodford Bourne)
Warre's Traditional 81 (bottled 1985) (Febvre, Searsons)

Aged Tawny Port

'True' tawny is aged in barrels for at least five but up to forty years; this explains the light amber colour of the wine, which is delicate and fragrant. The label indicates the oldest wine used in the blend. Delicious raisiny nutty flavours and aromas.
Cockburn's Tawny 10-year-old (Grants)
Croft Distinction Tawny Reserve (Gilbeys)
Dow's Tawny 10-year-old (James Adams)
Dow's Tawny 10-year-old (Karwig)
Fonseca Tawny 10, 20 or 40-year-old (Mitchells)
Ferreira Quinta do Porto 10-year-old Tawny (Reynolds)
Ferreira Duque de Bragarca 20-year-old Tawny (Reynolds)

Osborne Tawny (Barry & Fitzwilliam)
Warre's Nimrod Very Finest Old Tawny (Searsons)

Vintage character

A late-bottled vintage style blended from a number of years and aged in wood for five years. Having thrown their deposit in the bottle, the wines need not be decanted. Christmas cake aromas and flavours are stamped on these robust wines.

Cálem Vintage Character (Cassidy)
Churchill Finest Vintage Character (Findlater)
Delaforce Rich Vintage Character (United Beverages)
Dow's A.J.S. Vintage Character (James Adams)
Dow's Vintage Character (Karwig)
Fonseca Bin 27 (Vintage Character) (Mitchells)
Warre's Warrior Finest Vintage Character (Febvre)

Ruby Port

A blended uncomplicated style, aged for a few years. Sweet with mouth-filling flavour reminiscent of plum pudding: high-alcohol finish.

Cálem Ruby (Cassidy)
Cockburn's Fine Ruby (Grants)
Ferriera (Reynolds)
Ferriera Ruby (Karwig)
Fonseca Ruby (Mitchells)
Graham's Fine Ruby (Fitzgeralds)
Osborne Ruby (Barry & Fitzwilliam)
Offley Fine Ruby (Allied Drinks)
Sandeman 3 Star Fine Ruby (Dillons)
Warre's Fine Selected Ruby (Febvre)

White Port

May be dry or sweet. Dry white Port is good as an apéritif. High in alcohol and thick in texture, it benefits from being served very chilled.

Churchill White (Findlaters)
Croft (Gilbeys)
Ferreira Dry White (Reynolds)

Fonseca Sirocco (Mitchells)
Offley Extra Dry White (Allied Drinks)
Warre's Fine Selected White (Searsons)

If you find it difficult to locate vintage Port, try O'Briens of Donnybrook, Dublin 4, who carry an extensive range.

VINS DOUX NATURELS (VDN)

This is the term used to describe the fortified sweet dessert wines from the South of France. To produce a VDN, grape spirit is added to stop fermentation at an early stage. This results in a naturally sweet wine with an alcohol content ranging from 15 to 21%. White VDN, are produced from the Muscat grape while dark/red ones are produced from Grenache.

The following examples were tasted and highly rated by the panel:

Muscat de Beaumes-de-Venise from Chapoutier (Grants), Jaboulet (Gilbeys), Duboeuf (James Adams): The aroma and flavours of Muscat and a rich expansive fruit finish that goes on and on.

Domaine de la Rectorie Banyuls (Brangan): Deep purple with aromas of raisins, plums and caramel. Smooth in texture backed up with good alcohol. A delicious uncloying sweetness remains on the palate.

Muscat de Frontignan (Dunnes Stores): Honeyed golden dessert wine. Marmalade aromas. Fat and weighty on the palate. Good zesty acidity.

Rimage Banyuls (Mitchells): Light golden amber with silky smooth dried plum and fig tones. Flavours open out on the palate and finish in a smooth concentrated flourish.

Setúbal

Setúbal is a fortified wine from Portugal with its own DOC produced from the Moscatel (Muscat). After fortification the grape skins are left in contact with the wine for several months to enhance the grapey flavours. It is then aged in oak casks for several years before bottling. A good example is *Fonseca Setúbal* (Mitchells)

Wine Importers

Adam, James, 1 Charleston Rd, Dublin 6 Tel (01) 496 3143
  Fax (01) 496 0186

Allied Drinks Ltd, Merchants' Yard, East Wall Road,
  Dublin 1 Tel (01) 836 6898 Fax (01) 874 3998
  Windsor Hill House, Glounthane, Co Cork
  Tel (021) 353 438 Fax (021) 354 362

Barry & Fitzwilliam, Glanmire, Cork
  Tel (021) 821 555 Fax (021) 821 604
  50 Dartmouth Sq, Dublin 6
  Tel (01) 660 6984/66 Fax (01) 660 0479

Best Cellars, Coill Bhuí, 4 Knocklyon Road, Dublin 16
  Tel (01) 494 6508/088 598 516 Fax (01) 494 6508

Brangan and Co Ltd, 7 Deerpark Avenue, Dublin 15
  Tel/Fax (01) 821 4052

Burgundy Direct, 8 Monaloe Way, Blackrock, Co Dublin
  Tel (01) 289 6615/288 6239 Fax (01) 289 8470

Callaghan Wines, 19 Maywood Lawn, Raheny, Dublin 5
  Tel (01) 831 1369

Cassidy Wines Ltd, Unit 1B, Stillorgan Industrial Park,
  Co Dublin Tel (01) 295 4157

Delitalia, 'Oenotria', 35 Churchview Drive, Killiney,
  Co Dublin Tel (01) 285 4216

Dennison, David, Fine Wines, The Wine Vault, High Street,
  Waterford Tel/Fax (051) 53444

Dillon, Edward, & Co Ltd, 25 Mountjoy Sq, Dublin 1
  Tel (01) 836 4399 Fax (01) 878 6502

Dunnes Stores, Head Office, 67 Upper Stephen St, Dublin 8
  Tel (01) 475 1111 Fax (01) 475 1441

Ecock Wine & Spirit Merchants, Unit 3 Newpark Centre, Newtownpark Ave, Blackrock, Co Dublin
Tel (01) 283 1664

Febvre & Co. Limited, 60 Stillorgan Industrial Park, Blackrock, Co Dublin Tel (01) 295 9030 Fax (01) 295 9036

Findlaters (Wine Merchants) Ltd, The Harcourt Street Vaults, 10 Upper Hatch Street, Dublin 2
Tel (01) 475 1699 Fax (01) 475 2530

Fitzgerald and Co, 11–12 Bow St, Dublin 7
Tel (01) 872 5911 Fax (01) 872 2809

Foley Eurowine Ltd, 33 Johnstown Road, Dublin 18
Tel (01) 285 0026 Fax (01) 284 0671

Gilbeys of Ireland, Gilbey House, Belgard Rd, Dublin 24
Tel (01) 459 7444 Fax 459 0188

Grand Cru Wines Ltd, 48 Roches Street, Limerick
Tel (061) 417 784 Fax (061) 417 276

Grants of Ireland, St Lawrence Road, Chapelizod, Dublin 20 Tel (01) 626 4455 Fax (01) 626 4680

Greenhills Wines,   , Greenhills Road, Dublin 12

Hugan Wines, 21 Idrone Drive, Knockylon, Dublin 16
Tel (01) 494 5871

Jenkinson Wines, 6 Brooklawn Ave, Blackrock, Co Dublin
Tel (01) 288 3710

Karwig Wines, Kilnagleary, Carrigaline, Co Cork
Tel/Fax (021) 372 864

Kelly and Co (Dublin), 89 Gardiner St Dublin 1
Tel (01) 873 2100 Fax (01) 874 2245

MacCormaic Vintners, 43 Templeroan Park, Dublin 16
Tel (01) 494 1234

Mackenway Distributors, 27 Farmleigh Close, Stillorgan, Co Dublin Tel (01) 288 9010 Fax (01) 288 3830

Mitchell & Son, Wine Merchants, 21 Kildare Street, Dublin 2
Tel (01) 676 0766 Fax (01) 661 1509

Moore's Wines, 26 South Hill, Dartry, Dublin 6
Tel (01) 496 7617 Fax (01) 497 8142

Musgraves Ltd, St Margaret's Road, Dublin 11
Tel (01) 842 0944

Nicholson, James, 27A Killyleagh St, Crossgar, Co Down
Tel (0396) 830 091

Parsons, Kevin, Wines Ltd, 21 Liosbourne, Carrigaline, Co
Cork Tel/Fax (021) 373 237

Quinnsworth, Head Office, Gresham House, Marine Road,
Dun Laoghaire, Co Dublin Tel (01) 280 8441

Remy Ireland Ltd, 101 Monkstown Rd, Monkstown, Co
Dublin, Tel (01) 280 4341

Reynolds T. P. & Co, 50 Pembroke Rd, Dublin 4
Tel (01) 660 0246

Searsons Wine Merchants, 6a The Crescent, Monkstown,
Co Dublin Tel (01) 280 0405 Fax (01) 280 4771

Superquinn Support Office, Sutton, Dublin 13
Tel (01) 832 5700

Syrah Wines Ltd, 11 Rowanbyrn, Blackrock, Co Dublin,
Tel (01) 289 3670 Fax (01) 289 3306

Taserra Wine Merchants, Hogan House, Grand Canal St,
Dublin 2 Tel (01) 490 0537 Fax (01) 490 4052

Terroirs, 103 Morehampton Road, Donnybrook, Dublin 4
Tel (01) 667 1311 Fax (01) 667 1312

United Beverages, Finches Industrial Park, Long Mile
Road, Dublin 12 Tel (01) 450 2000 Fax (01) 450 9004

Valcomino, Unit 46, Coolmine Ind. Estate, Clonsilla,
Dublin 15 Tel (01) 820 9192 Fax (01) 820 9151

Wines Direct, Tel 1800–579 579 Fax (044) 40015

Woodford Bourne, 79 Broomhill Road Tallaght,
Dublin 24 Tel (01) 459 9000 Fax (01) 459 9342

Wine Retailers

The major supermarket chains all have off-licence departments. We have listed below other outlets specialising in wine.

Mail/Tel Order

Burgundy Direct Tel (01) 289 6615/288 6239
  Fax (01) 289 8470
Delitalia Tel (01) 285 4216
Wines Direct, Freefone Tel 1800-579579 Fax (044) 40015
Best Cellars, Coill Bhuí, 4 Knocklyon Road, Dublin 16
  Tel (01) 494 6508/088 598 516 Fax (01) 494 6508

Antrim

Direct Wine Shipments, 5/7 Corporation Square, Belfast
  BT1 Tel (0232) 238 700
Supermac, Newtownbreda Shopping Centre, Saintfield
  Rd, Belfast BT8 Tel (0232) 491 176
Wine Gallery, Boucher Rd, Belfast BT12 Tel (0232) 231 231

Carlow

Tully's Wine Shop, 148 Tullow St, Co. Carlow
  Tel (0503) 42660

Cavan

Kangley, Patrick, Main St, Bailieborough, Co Cavan
  Tel (042) 65480
Blessing's Off Licence, Pearse Street, Cavan Tel (049) 31138

Clare

Knight's Liquor Store, Shannon Knight's Inn, Shannon,
  Co Clare Tel (061) 361 045 Fax (061) 361 596

Cork

Bishopstown Off Licence, Bishopstown, Cork
  Tel (021) 541 151
Bradley's Off Licence, North Main Street, Cork
  Tel (021) 270 845

Centra Off Licence, Main Street, Dunmanway, Co Cork

Clifford's Off Licence, 91 Shandon Street, Cork
Tel (021) 304 555

Clifton Off Licence, Canon O'Leary Place, Cobh, Co Cork

Daily's Off Licence, Village Green, Douglas, Cork
Tel (021) 891 733

Desmond's Off Licence, South Main Street, Bandon, Co
Cork

Fine Wines Ltd, 64 Patrick St, Cork Tel (021) 270 273

Foley's Off Licence, 28 Bridge St, Mallow, Co Cork Tel
(022) 21480

Galvins, Washington St, Cork Tel (021) 276 314; Clermont
Road, Douglas, Cork Tel (021) 291 100; 37 Bandon Rd,
The Lough, Cork Tel (021) 316 098

Half Door, The, Bandon, Co Cork

Karwig Wines, Kilnagleary, Carrigaline, Co Cork
Tel/Fax (021) 372 864

Lynch's Off Licence, Glanmire, Co Cork

Mansfield's Off Licence, Patrick Street, Fermoy, Co Cork

Pomeroys Wine Cellar, 21 South Mall, Cork
Tel (021) 274 753

Paisley's Super Valu, Youghal, Co Cork

Super Valu, Blarney, Co Cork Tel (021) 385 571

Super Valu, Main Street, Carrigaline, Co Cork

Super Valu, Strand Street, Kanturk, Co Cork

Wine Fare, 19 Patrick St, Fermoy, Co Cork Tel (025) 31031

Donegal

Gethings, Thomas, Upper Main Street, Dungloe, Co
Donegal Tel (075) 21014

McGarry's Off Licence, High Road, Letterkenny, Co
Donegal

Off Licence, Donegal Town, Co Donegal

Port Off Licence, Port Road, Letterkenny, Co Donegal

Super Valu Off Licence, Raphoe, Co Donegal

Down

Nicholson, James, 27A Killyleagh St, Crossgar, Co Down
Tel (01396) 830 091

The Ava, 132 Main St, Bangor, Co Down

Tel (0247) 465 490

Dublin

Acheson's Off Licence, 20 Errigal Road, Crumlin, Dublin 12 Tel (01) 455 7358

Best Cellar Off Licence/Wine Shop, Coolock Village, Dublin 5 Tel (01) 867 1181

Boland's Wine Market, 169 St Mobhi Road, Drumcondra, Dublin 9 Tel (01) 837 3220

Bracken's Off Licence, 191 Botanic Road, Dublin 9 Tel (01) 837 3467

Carolan's Off Licence, 12 Upper Sherrard Street, Dublin 7

Carville's Off Licence, 39 Lower Camden Street, Dublin 2 Tel (01) 475 1791

Cheers, Butterfield Ave, Rathfarnham, Dublin 14 Tel (01) 494 6705

Cheers Howth, Main Street, Howth Tel (01) 832 2691

Christine's Off Licence, 3 Berkeley Road, Dublin 7 Tel (01) 830 2118

Cooney's, 197 Harold's Cross Road, Dublin 6W Tel (01) 497 1761

Cork's Food and Drink, 116 Terenure Rd North, Dublin 6 Tel (01) 490 5264

Creggy's Off Licence, 151 Emmet Road, Dublin Road

Deveney's Off-Licence

16 Upper Rathmines Road Dublin 6 Tel (01) 497 2392

294/296 Harolds Cross Dublin 6 Tel (01) 492 3092

31 Main Street, Dundrum, Dublin 14 Tel (01) 298 4288

Rosemount Shopping Centre, Rathfarnham, Dublin 14 Tel (01) 493 6918

106 Rathgar Road, Dublin 6 Tel (01) 497 2392

Dolphin's Barn, Tel (01) 453 4932

New Sandyford SC, Balally Tel (01) 295 7237

Donnybrook Fair, 89 Morehampton Rd, Donnybrook, Dublin 4 Tel (01) 668 3556

Douglas Food Co, 53 Donnybrook Road, Dublin 4 Tel (01) 269 4066 Fax (01) 269 4492

Eugene's Off Licence, Edenmore Road, Dublin 5

Farm Produce, 17 Upper Baggot Street, Dublin 2 Tel (01) 668 5596

Findlater's (Wine Merchants) Ltd, The Harcourt Street
Vaults, 10 Upper Hatch Street, Dublin 2
Tel (01) 475 1699 Fax (01) 475 2530

Fitzgerald's Off Licence, 151 Rathgar Road, Dublin 6

Foley's Fine Wines, 33A Johnstown Rd, Cabinteely, Dublin 18
Tel (01) 285 0026 Fax (01) 284 0671

Fox's Off Licence, 1 Millmount Terrace, Drumcondra,
Dublin 9

Gammells, 33 Ranelagh, Dublin 6 Tel (01) 496 2311

Goggin's Off Licence, 99 Monkstown Road, Monkstown
Co Dublin

Gourmet Shop, 48 Highfield Road, Dublin 6

Groome's Off Licence, 33A Ashtown Grove, Navan Road,
Dublin 9

Hallinan's Off Licence, 4 Military Road, Ballybrack,
Co Dublin

Higgins Off Licence, 34 Gledswood Drive, Clonskeagh,
Co Dublin Tel (01) 269 7276

Italian Food Shop, 37 Dunville Avenue, Dublin 6
Tel (01) 497 3411 Fax (01) 496 2752

JC's Supermarket, Swords Shopping Centre, Rathkeale,
Swords, Co Dublin Tel (01) 840 2884

Jus de Vine, Unit 10, Portmarnock Town Centre, Co Dublin
Tel (01) 846 1192

Kehoe's Supermarket, 129-131 Ballymun Road, Dublin 9

Kelly's Off Licence, Malahide Rd, Artane, Dublin 5
Tel (01) 831 1867

Kelly's Wine Cellar, 39 Phibsboro Rd, Dublin 7
Tel (01) 830 4942

Kenny & Sons Limited Off Licence, 133 Galtymore Road,
Dublin 12 Tel (01) 4557324

Lord Mayor's, The, Swords

Magic Carpet, Cornelscourt, Foxrock, Dublin 18
Tel (01) 289 5678

Martin's Off Licence, 11 Marino Mart, Dublin 3
Tel (01) 833 2952

May's Off Licence, 32 Infirmary Road, Dublin 7
Tel (01) 677 3515

Mc Cormack's Off Licence, 176 South Circular Road Dublin

8 Tel (01) 8453 4054

McCabes Wine Merchants, 51–55 Mount Merrion Ave, Blackrock, Co Dublin Tel (01) 288 2037

Vernon Avenue, Clontarf, Dublin 3 Tel (01) 833 5277

McCaughey's Off Licence, 13 Clonliffe Road, Dublin 3 Tel (01) 837 5266

McHughs, 57 Kilbarrack Road Tel (01) 834 4692

Mitchell's Wine Shop, 21 Kildare Street, Dublin 2 Tel (01) 676 0766 Fax (01) 661 1509

Molloys Off-Licence,

Village Green, Tallaght, Dublin 24 Tel (01) 451 4857

Orchard Road, Clondalkin Tel (01) 457 0166

Crumlin Shopping Centre Tel (01) 453 1611

Ballymun Shopping Centre Tel (01) 842 8189

Main Street, Blanchardstown Tel (01) 821 0129

Ballygall Road West, Finglas Tel (01) 864 0251

Nutgrove Shopping Centre Tel (01) 493 6077

Mortons Supermarket, Dunville Avenue, Ranelagh, Dublin 6 Tel (01)497 1254/497 1913 Fax (01) 497 1978

Murphy's Off Licence, 514 South Circular Road, Dublin 8

Nolan's Supermarket, 49 Vernon Ave, Clontarf, Dublin 3 Tel (01) 833 8361

O'Brien's Fine Wines,

30–32 Donnybrook Rd, Dublin 4 Tel (01) 269 3033

Carysfort Avenue, Blackrock Tel (01) 288 1649

Unit 4, 22 Sandymount Green Tel (01) 668 2096

Castle St, Dalkey Tel (01) 285 8944

58 Georges St Upper, Dun Laoghaire Tel (01) 280 6952

O'Lorcain Off Licence, 59 Dublin St, Balbriggan, Co Dublin Tel (01) 841 2309

Palette, 67 Main St, Blackrock, Co Dublin Tel (01) 283 4530

Quinn's Off Licence 50 Lower Drumcondra Road, Dublin 9 Tel (01) 830 5858

Raynestonn Limited, 71 Fairview Strand, Dublin 3

Redmonds, 25 Ranelagh Village, Dublin 6 Tel (01) 496 0552/497 1739 Fax (01) 497 8533

Reid & Sons Limited Off Licence,115 Cabra Road, Dublin 7

Savage, J.C., Swords Shopping Centre

Searsons Wine Merchants, 6a The Crescent, Monkstown,

Co Dublin Tel (01) 280 0405

Shiels Off Licence, 62 Lower Dorset Street, Dublin 1 Tel (01) 830 7497

Slattery's Off Licence, Dunville Avenue, Rathmines, Dublin 6 Tel (01) 497 4341

Super Valu Off Licence, Bayside Shopping Centre, Sutton Dublin 13

Sweeney's Off Licence, 20 Lr Dorset Street, Dublin 1 Tel (01) 874 9808

Terroirs, 103 Morehampton Road, Donnybrook, Dublin 4 Tel (01) 667 1311 Fax (01) 667 1312

Thomas's, Brighton Rd, Foxrock, Dublin 18

Verlings Wines, 360 Clontarf Rd, Dublin 3 Tel (01) 833 1653

Village Winery, Main Street, Swords, Co Dublin

Vine Tree Off Licence, 82 Ballybough Road, Dublin 3 Tel (01) 836 3322

Vintage, The, Newpark Centre, Newtown Park Avenue, Blackrock, Co Dublin Tel (01) 283 1664

149 Rathmines Road Upper, Dublin 6 Tel (01) 496 7811

Vintry, The, 102 Rathgar Road Dublin 6 Tel/Fax (01) 490 5477

Wine Cellar, Raheny Shopping Centre, Howth Road, Dublin 5 Tel (01) 830 4942

Galway

"98" Off licence, Prospect Hill, Galway

McCambridge's 38/39 Shop Street Galway Tel (091) 62259/63470 Fax (091) 61276

McInerney's Off Licence, Loughrea, Co Galway

Merchant's Wine Club, The Cornstore, Middle Street, Galway Tel (091) 561 833

Vineyard Off Licence, 14 Mainguard Street, Galway

Kerry

Garvey's Off Licence, Dingle, Co Kerry Tel (066) 51397/ (066) 51649

Kildare

Dunne's Off Licence, Woodstock Street, Athy, Co Kildare

Boyle, John, Limited, Market Square, Kildare

Mill Wine Cellar, Mill Street, Maynooth, Co Kildare
Tel (01) 628 9520

Kilkenny

Wine Centre, 15 John St, Kilkenny, Tel (056) 22034

Limerick

Fine Wines Limerick,
Vintage House, 48 Roche's St, Limerick Tel (061) 417784
Fax (061) 417276
Ambassador Centre, Cork Rd, Dooradoyle, Limerick
N. Portley Off Licence, Round House, High Street,
Limerick
Railway Wines, 39 Parnell Street, Limerick
Wine Cellar, The Elms, Ennis Rd, Limerick

Louth

Admiral's Off Licence, 36 Shop Street, Drogheda, Co Louth
Tel (041) 31350
Callan, 40 Park Street, Dundalk, Co Louth (042) 34382
Egan's Off-Licence, 1 Peter St, Drogheda, Co Louth
Tel (041) 31810
Hanratty's Off Licence, 65 Scarlett Street, Drogheda,
Co Louth Tel (041) 37122
McAllister Off Licence, 65 Bridge Street, Dundalk,
Co Louth
MJ Bars Limited, 65 Park Street, Dundalk, Co Louth
Tel (042) 34463
Super Valu, Off Licence Section, Ardee, Co Louth
Tel (041) 53322
Tenanty & Sons Ltd, Market Street, Ardee, Co Louth
Tel (041) 53820

Mayo

Tuffy, Bohensup, Ballina, Co. Mayo Tel (096) 21300

Meath

Off Licence, 53 Academy Street, Navan, Co Meath
Off Licence, Market Square, Navan, Co Meath
Reilly's Off Licence, 51 Claremount Street, Navan,

Co Meath

Smyth's Off Licence, Railway Street, Navan, Co Meath

Sligo

The Wine Barrel, Johnston Court, Sligo Tel (071) 71730

Tipperary

Bernie's Super Valu, Roscrea, Co Tipperary

Castlehyperstore, 47 Pearse St, Nenagh, Co Tipperary Tel (067) 31444

Lonergan's Off Licence, 36 O'Connell St, Clonmel, Co Tipperary Tel (052) 21250

Waterford

Dennison, David, Fine Wines, The Wine Vault, High Street, Waterford Tel/Fax (051) 53444

L&N Superstores, Parnell St, Dungarvan, Co Waterford Tel (058) 41628

L&N, Priest's Road, Tramore, Co Waterford Tel (051) 386 036

Westmeath

Old Stand Off Licence, 48 Dominick Street, Mullingar, Co Westmeath

Wexford

Caulfield Supermarket Ltd, 17 Irishtown, New Ross, Co Wexford Tel (051) 22101

W Gaynor & Sons Off Licence, Wygram Place, Wexford Tel (053) 22061

Wicklow

O'Brien's Fine Wines,
  19 Quinnsboro Road, Bray, Co Wicklow Tel (01) 286 3732
  2 Vevay Arcade, Bray, Co Wicklow Tel (01) 286 8776
  Church Road, Greystones, Co Wicklow Tel (01) 287 4123